Exclusive Distributors
Music Sales Limited,
8/9 Frith Street,
London W1D 3JB, UK.

Music Sales Corporation,
257 Park Avenue South,
New York, NY 10010, USA.

Macmillan Distribution Services,
53 Park West Drive,
Derrimut, Vic 3030,
Australia.

To the Music Trade only:
Music Sales Limited,
8/9 Frith Street,
London W1D 3JB, UK.

A catalogue record for this book is available
from the British Library.

Visit Omnibus Press on the web at www.omnibuspress.com

The Elvis Archives

OMNIBUS PRESS

London/New York/Paris/Sydney/Copenhagen/Berlin/Madrid/Tokyo

INTRODUCTION

If you travel about a hundred miles south-east from Memphis, you'll arrive in Tupelo, Mississippi, the birthplace of Elvis Presley.

Tupelo is a relatively laid back sort of place, which exudes oodles of Southern hospitality. It is a magnet for Elvis fans worldwide: come, see the little two-room, white-painted wooden house, refurbished Thirties style and set in beautifully landscaped grounds. There is a memorial chapel, dedicated in 1979, and an Elvis museum dating from the early Nineties. A bronze statue of Elvis aged 13 was unveiled in January, 2002, and dedicated to fans worldwide on the 25th anniversary in August that year. A "story wall" was added in 2003 with plaques bearing quotes from local people who knew Elvis. The wall is dark brown in colour, to accentuate the white birthplace, and incorporates a "Fountain of Life" commemorating Elvis's Tupelo years. Also added in 2003, and encircling the birthplace, is a sidewalk with a stone for every year of Elvis's life.

It is evident that the Elvis Presley Memorial Foundation and the good folk of Tupelo have immense pride in their native son.

Right: Elvis the Hillbilly Cat

4

CONTENTS

CHAPTER 1
"IN THE GHETTO"

It was very different back in 1935 on that cold January day – the 8th, a Tuesday – when Gladys Love Presley, aged 22, gave birth to identical twins in the tiny house on Old Saltillo Road built by Vernon Presley, his father, and his brother Vester. Vernon was four years younger than his wife, and they'd only moved into their new home the previous month.

Sadness mingled with joy; the first child, Jessie Garon, was stillborn. Happily, Elvis Aaron survived and was given love in abundance. There may have been dreadful poverty and hardship in East Tupelo in the Depression-hit Thirties, but love cost nothing, and Tupelo's child grew up secure in the heart of his family, and in a church-minded, close-knit community that sang its heart out in praise of God. The music the boy heard in the First Assembly of God church was to influence and shape his future. A quote in early fanzines, attributed to Gladys, told how the church singing affected her young son: "When Elvis was about two years old, he'd slide off my lap, run down the aisle, and stand looking up at the choir and try to sing with them. He was

Even then, he couldn't stand still when he sang

too little to know the words, but he could carry the tune."

As he grew older, Elvis sang at church revivals with his parents, a favourite song being, 'I Won't Have To Cross The Jordan Alone'. "Even then," Gladys reportedly said, "he couldn't stand still when he sang." Interestingly, the only Grammys that Elvis ever won were for gospel music (in 1967 for the album *How Great Thou Art*, in 1972 for the album *He Touched Me*, and in 1974 for a live performance of 'How Great Thou Art'). In 2001, Elvis was inducted posthumously into the Gospel Music Hall of Fame, whose previous inductees included Mahalia Jackson and Billy Graham.

The pastor of the First Assembly of God church in East Tupelo was Frank Smith, who used a guitar and sang to get his message across to his congregation, and who encouraged young Elvis in his singing.

HUMBLE ORIGINS

Many years after Elvis became famous, it became known that Vernon Presley had done time in Parchman Penitentiary in Mississippi. With two others, he'd forged a cheque, and in June 1938, began his three-year incarceration, but was released in less than a year. The loss of the main family breadwinner meant that Gladys and Elvis had to leave their home and move in with relatives. On Vernon's release, the family lived in a succession of homes. Gladys, a skilled needlewoman, did her bit to help the family finances, and Vernon found what work he could.

Left: Elvis and his parents, Gladys and Vernon, in 1937.

In the autumn of 1941, six-year-old Elvis began to attend East Tupelo Consolidated School on Lake Street, also known as Lawhon Elementary School. One of his classmates was Becky Martin, who recalled that pupils were required to learn the names of the American presidents and the capital cities of each state, as well as the Gettysburg Address, the one that contains the oft-quoted words, "… government of the people, for the people, by the people", which Abraham Lincoln gave in 1862.

Like Elvis, Becky Martin enjoyed singing. Before classes at Lawhon School, Becky said that there'd be a chapel service, and Elvis would sometimes sing 'God Bless My Daddy', or say a prayer. It was, some sources say, Elvis's 5th grade teacher, Mrs Oleta Grimes, who taught Elvis to sing 'Old Shep', a touching ballad about a boy and his faithful dog. She certainly had plenty of faith in the quiet child, and in 1945, when he was ten years old, it was Mrs Grimes who entered the shy lad into the Children's Day contest at the annual Mississippi-Alabama fair at the Tupelo Fairgrounds on October 3. One of many Presley myths is that he came second. It wasn't so. Elvis himself recalled that he was placed fifth, which entitled him to free rides on the fairground attractions. He performed 'Old Shep', which he'd record in 1956 for his second album but which he steadfastly refused to sing on stage in the Seventies, no matter how often audiences might request it.

Believe it or not, an extremely rare photo surfaced in Bill E. Burk's 1994 book, *The Tupelo Years*. Black and white, and somewhat grainy, it shows the talent contest winners and runners-up lined up on stage. Elvis, wearing spectacles, his pants held up by braces, has his hands behind his back. The winning contestant, Shirley Gillentine, runner-up, (Miss) Nubin Payne, and third prize-winner – a tall, unknown boy – all proudly display their trophies.

Right: Elvis aged 6. His first school photograph

'Old Shep' was written by Red Foley, well-known in the country music field. In rural Tupelo, country & western would have been another type of music that Elvis heard and was influenced by. To a lesser extent, he'd have heard the blues, and after the family moved to North Green Street, near the centre of town, in 1946, the hand-clapping revivalist meetings at the local "coloured" church would have made a deep impression on him.

Even though Gladys kept a close eye on him, out of school and away from church Elvis enjoyed forbidden pleasures, as many a young lad would. His friend Odell

Dreaming, imagining, but never in his wildest dreams knowing where his passion for music would lead him

Clark has recalled that Elvis wasn't supposed to go into the woods, but he'd slip out from under his mother's watchful eye and, with his young, conspiratorial chums, ride home-made wagons made from apple crates down a slalom course in the wooded hills. In his backyard, another friend, Guy Harris, remembered that Elvis had a "flying jenny", a board nailed onto a post, and he and his friends would swing round and round on it. Store bought, expensive toys and games weren't affordable for most East Tupelo families. Even so, folks who knew Elvis recalled that he often gave

away whatever toys he had to other children.

But when it came to his peanut butter and crackers, whenever his Uncle Vester, Vernon's older brother, came around, little Elvis would urgently advise Gladys to hide the food from his uncle, who had teased him about stealing the peanut butter and crackers.

As he grew older Elvis enjoyed going to the movies and, for 50 cents, watching favourite heroes like Flash Gordon, Gene Autry and Roy Rogers up there on the silver screen. As the youngster followed them through their thrilling adventures, maybe he imagined what it would be like to be a movie star…

The day before Elvis celebrated his 11th birthday, a small tornado ripped through Tupelo. The area can experience extremes of weather, from unbelievably hot, humid summers, to damaging winter ice storms. Tornados are an occasional regional hazard.

GUITAR MAN

For his birthday, as a gift from his parents, he chose an acoustic guitar. The Tupelo Hardware Store on Main Street, where the guitar was purchased from a Mr Forrest L. Bobo, is famous to this day, and is visited by thousands of fans. The owners are proud of their Elvis connection.

It's easy to imagine young, blond, tow-headed Elvis sitting around on his family porch and trying to master the rudiments of guitar playing. Dreaming, imagining, but never in his wildest dreams knowing where his passion for music would lead him. What tunes did he practice, and maybe sing along to? He was tutored by the youthful church pastor, Frank Smith, and by his uncle, Johnny Smith, Gladys's brother. Frank Smith took Elvis and others to the green-domed Tupelo Courthouse on Saturday afternoons, where the WELO Jamboree, an amateur radio show, was broadcast. It was here that Elvis met and was encouraged by a popular singer who called himself "Mississippi Slim".

In 1946, Elvis commenced at Milam Junior High School in Tupelo, entering the 6th grade. There's a photo of his 6th grade class in which he looks very much out of place, the only pupil wearing overalls. Many years hence, at a show in Las Vegas on December 11, 1976, a woman handed Elvis a pair of blue denim overalls. "Honey," he told her in a voice of mock disgust, "I left those in Mississippi 200 years ago," adding that he'd tried to avoid overalls all his life. "Honey, I can't put them on. You've got to be kiddin' me."

Music – everything from the country songs he heard on the Grand Ole Opry radio broadcasts to church hymns –

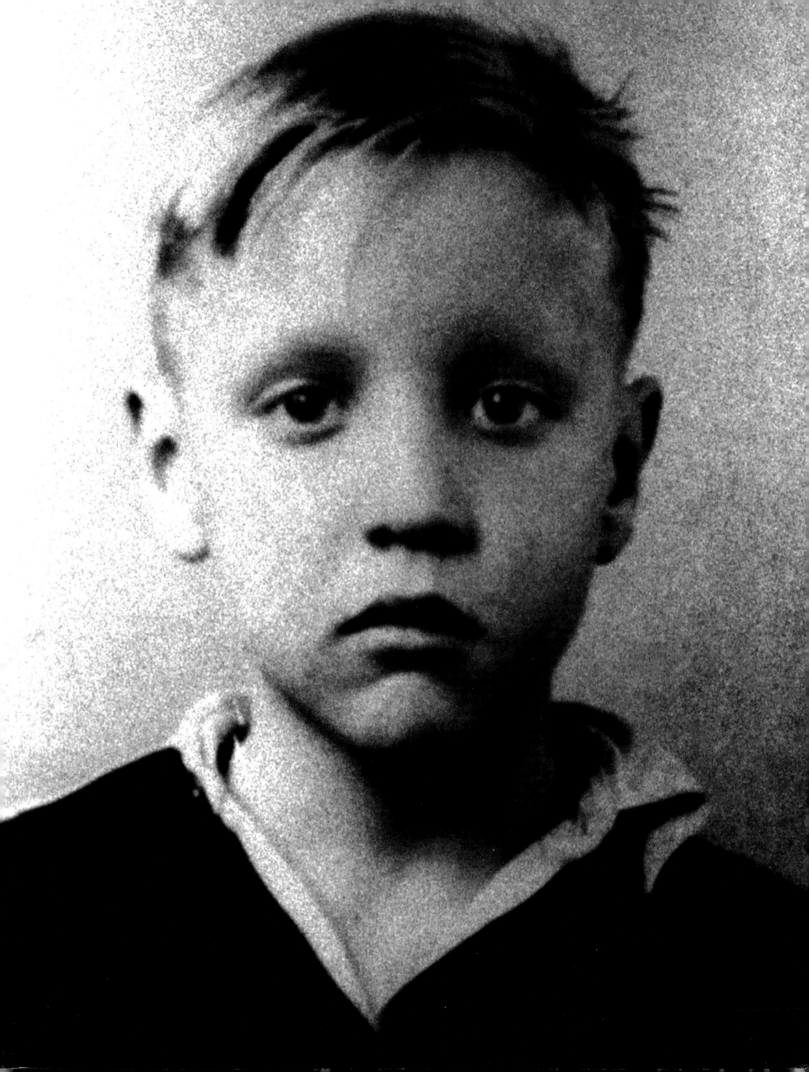

continued to enthuse Elvis. By 7th grade at Milam he was taking his guitar to school daily, strumming away in the lunch hour and break periods, albeit failing to impress his classmates to any great extent. While he was in the 8th grade, which he began in September 1948, school bullies cut the strings of his guitar, but classmates rallied round and collected enough to buy him new ones.

Left: Outside Lauderdale courts, Memphis, with a toy gun, 1950

The few photos that exist of Elvis during the time he lived in Tupelo give very little inkling of the devastatingly handsome looks that would wow millions of female fans once he became a worldwide phenomenon.

Times remained tough in Tupelo. While Gladys worked as a seamstress, Vernon tried his hand at different jobs, and several times lived temporarily in other areas where work was available. One time, in May 1943, the whole family relocated to the Mississippi Gulf Coast, where Vernon had found work in a shipyard. After only a few weeks, they returned to Tupelo, homesick. Presley senior was regularly taking out loans and borrowing money. Finally, in early November, 1948, the little family packed their meagre belongings – including Elvis's beloved guitar – into a 1939 Plymouth car, heading north-west to Memphis along the two-lane blacktop roller-coaster Highway 78, a road that would one day bear the name, "The Elvis Aaron Presley Memorial Highway". Of the move to Tennessee and an uncertain future, Gladys Presley is on record as saying, "Things just had to be better".

Nowadays, a fast, modern, multi-lane highway links

Above: Elvis aged 13 (Tupelo Photographic Studio)

their little white house.

If you really want to trace Elvis's roots, then Tupelo is where you have to go. It has grown and prospered since the days when a dark-blond young lad sat on the steps of his family's home, let his fingers ripple over the strings of his guitar, and dreamed of what might be.

If you get the opportunity to travel to America's deep South then make sure that you spend some time in Tupelo, talk to the local people, and you'll find a

Elvis Presley always remained down-to-earth, friendly, and approachable

thriving Tupelo to Memphis's urban sprawl, and during the renovations to the birthplace grounds in 2003, a car similar to the Presleys' '39 Plymouth was located in Pennsylvania and brought to Tupelo, restored, and placed on show near

caring, God-fearing community. Only then will you understand why Elvis Presley always remained down-to-earth, friendly, and approachable despite all his wealth, fame, and superstardom.

11

CHAPTER 2
"I'M JUST A COUNTRY BOY, LONELY AND BLUE"

The large, bustling city of Memphis, located in the south-west corner of Tennessee only a few miles north of the Mississippi state line, and with the wide, mighty Mississippi River to the west, forming the border with Arkansas, must have seemed both exciting and scary to the shy 13-year-old country boy from Tupelo.

After the family had found a temporary place to stay – a rooming house on Washington Street – Elvis had to face his first day in the 8th grade at LC Humes High School. Vernon walked his son there, but the teenager baulked at the sight of so large and imposing a building and hundreds of unfamiliar faces. Before long, he was back home. He made it on day two and was gradually assimilated into school life. There's a myth that Gladys walked her son to school daily, but rather, it seems that she followed him at a distance to see that he got there safely.

By June of 1949, the family had moved to another rooming house on Poplar Avenue (which was still standing in the Eighties, looking decidedly *Psycho*-esque), and Vernon had a job at United Paint loading cans. His wage of around $40 a week meant that the Presleys were eligible for public housing, and in September they moved into the Lauderdale Courts complex. Around this time, they began to attend a newly-built church on 7th Street pastured by the Reverend Rex Dyson. Elvis also attended Sunday school there, where he was taught by Marion Carson. Mr Dyson, who lived to over 100 years of age, recalled baptizing Gladys, Vernon, and Elvis around 1950.

By the time he was 17 years old, Elvis had grown into a disarmingly handsome fellow, and his interest in music had intensified. He revelled in the music he heard in church. He listened to both gospel and country on the radio. He also heard blues-orientated music of the black R&B artists on local radio stations. He hung around with other, older teenagers at the Lauderdale Courts who played music, and learned from them.

Memphis was the perfect place to be for someone with Elvis' keen interest in music; after all, it was home to historic Beale Street with its bars and clubs where the blues were sung nightly. Beale Street was a magnet for Elvis.

While in the 10th grade at Humes in 1950, Elvis enlisted in the ROTC (Reserve Officers' Training Corps), and was pictured with other pupils, all proudly wearing their uniforms. In class, he got an "A" in English. Towards the end of the year, he found work as an usher in Loew's State Theatre on South Main Street, enjoying the chance to see all the movies that played there. By the middle of 1951, Elvis was doing a summer job at Precision Tool, where Vernon had previously worked, and during the year, Elvis took his driving test.

Right: Elvis aged 10 at the Tupelo Fair, 1945

The teenage Elvis was beginning to take more time and trouble over his appearance, growing his hair longer than

The teenage Elvis was beginning to take more time and trouble over his appearance

the norm – this was the era of crew cuts – and grooming it with Vaseline. He tried to grow sideburns and style his locks into a quiff. He started to patronise Lansky Brothers' outfitters on Beale Street, and told Bernard and Guy Lansky that he didn't care for hire purchase, but that, "When I have me some money, I'm gonna come in and buy you out". He kept that promise, purchasing many of his clothes from there after he found fame, and in doing so, helped make the store famous. A master salesman, Bernard

Lansky in later years welcomed the many fans who visited his shop. He continued to exploit his Elvis connection when Lanskys relocated to the Peabody Hotel in the mid-Nineties, even producing a special range of Presley-inspired clothing for the 25th anniversary in 2002.

As well as the Beale Street clubs Elvis could listen to blues and R&B by tuning into local radio stations. Late at night, there was Dewey Phillips – who'd later play a key role in Elvis's rise to fame – blasting out discs by the likes of Elmore James or Muddy Waters. On WDIA, an all black station, local bluesman BB King spun the platters.

Another DJ who would play a key role in Elvis's early fame was Bob Neal. On WMPS, he'd spin hillbilly music, or gospel from the Blackwood Brothers Quartet, now based in Memphis. These and other stations gave listeners a diverse choice of music, and Elvis listened to it all.

However, he didn't take his guitar to school, as he had in Tupelo, and he kept any musical aspirations mainly to himself, just playing around Lauderdale Courts with his like-minded friends.

Elvis continued to work after school to supplement the family budget, but his 3-11 pm shift at Marl Metal Products in September 1952 caused him to fall asleep in class, so he had to quit. Gladys was working at St Joseph's Hospital and Vernon at United Paint, and their combined income meant that they were no longer eligible to live at Lauderdale Courts. So on January 7, 1953, the day before Elvis' 18th birthday, they moved out, and lived for a few weeks at Saffarans Street, near Humes, then at 462 Alabama, not far from Lauderdale.

FIRST PERFORMANCE

A significant event took place on April 9: the Humes High School Minstrel Show in which Elvis took part. He was number 16 on a programme that included singers, dancers, band numbers, a tap dancer, an acrobat, and various instrumental solos. He was listed as a guitarist and his name misspelled as Elvis *Prestly*. The day of the show arrived – a Thursday – and as Elvis remembered it, "I wasn't popular in school. I wasn't dating anyone… and they entered me in this talent show and I came out and I did my first number, 'Cold, Cold Icy Fingers'". Elvis' performance garnered the most applause, and Mildred Scrivener, his home-room (form) teacher and the person who'd entered him into the show, told him to go out and do another song. "So I did. I sang 'Til I Waltz With You Again' [a hit for Teresa Brewer].

I heard a loud rumbling. It must have been applause." "*They really liked me, didn't they, Miss Scrivener?*'" was Elvis's surprised response. "It was really amazing how popular I became after that," he added. It must have surprised many of his classmates, who didn't know that he could sing.

Mildred Scrivener recalled that after his first "live" appearance, Elvis began to take his guitar around with him, and at a school picnic in Overton Park, he drew an audience as he sat playing guitar and singing plaintive ballads. He'd begun dating Regis Vaughan, and before the

"It was really amazing how popular I became"

school year ended, took her to the senior prom, held in the Peabody Hotel's ballroom. They also attended all-night singin's at Ellis Auditorium. The South Hall at Ellis Auditorium was the venue for a ceremony on June 3, when Elvis received his high school diploma, proudly watched by his parents. The diploma was soon framed and on show in their home. A prophecy in the Humes Yearbook for 1953 listed Elvis as one of a number of

Left: Elvis at June Juanico's Biloxi home, summer 1956

"singing hillbillies of the road". Little were they to know…

Before that, Elvis had to get a job. He showed up at the Memphis Employment Office the morning after his graduation and secured a temporary job as a machinist at M. B. Parker Company. Later in the year, he returned to Precision Tool.

Perhaps inspired by his success in the school show, sometime that summer Elvis went to the Memphis Recording Service to try out his voice on a private recording. Things were happening down at 706 Union Avenue, where Sam Phillips had formed Sun Records the previous year, of which the Memphis Recording Service (founded in 1950) was an adjunct. One of music's great visionaries, Sam was committed to recording black blues artists, and some of Sun's first releases had included Rufus Thomas's 'Tiger Man' and Little Junior's Blue Flames' 'Feelin' Good'. Sam had earlier recorded B. B. King, Rosco Gordon, and Howlin' Wolf on the Memphis Recording Service and sold their masters to established record companies. After 'Rocket 88' became a huge seller for Jackie Brenston in 1951, Sam decided to start Sun Records, and Elvis would have heard Dewey Phillips on

WHBQ raving about Sun's latest recordings.

It cost $8.25 to make a two-sided acetate, and that's just what Elvis did on July 15th 1953, telling receptionist Marian Keisker, who asked who he sounded like, that "I don't sound like nobody". He committed two ballads, 'My

I sang everything I knew pop, spirituals, anything I remembered

Happiness' and 'That's When Your Heartaches Begin', to wax, accompanying himself on guitar. He ventured that he wanted to surprise his mother with the disc, but it seems feasible that he hoped to catch Sam Phillips' ear. Some accounts have Sam at the studio on that hot Memphis Saturday; other accounts say that only Marian was there and that it was she who detected something special, something unusual in Elvis's voice, made a note to tell Sam, and managed to capture Elvis on tape to play back to her boss.

It's easy to imagine Elvis rushing home with his precious acetate and waiting to see Gladys's reaction. She would have no doubt been thrilled and proud.

A few months later, in January 1954, Elvis returned to 706 Union Avenue to record a second acetate. Sam Phillips was there, but he didn't show any special response to Elvis's two country ballads, 'I'll Never Stand In Your Way' and 'It Wouldn't Be The Same Without You'. Once more, Elvis picked up his acetate and took it home. He continued to turn up at Sun Studio over the next few months, Marian remembered.

TRUCK DRIVIN' MAN

Around this time, Elvis began to date Dixie Locke, and took her to the movies, to all-night gospel singin's at Ellis Auditorium, to Riverside and Overton Parks, and to his favourite hangouts around town. In May, they attended the annual Memphis Cotton Carnival. Elvis had begun to attend the First Assembly of God Church, where Dixie went to Sunday school, and where the Blackwood Brothers Quartet sang. Sometimes, though, they sneaked off to the nearby "coloured" church where the Reverend Herbert Brewster put fire into his preaching. That spring, Elvis auditioned unsuccessfully for The Songfellows, a junior

version of The Blackwoods. Many years later, he joked on stage in Las Vegas that he was rejected because he couldn't stand still! He changed jobs again, joining Crown Electric, where he drove a delivery truck and aspired to be an electrician. His employers were the Tiplers. At a show in as Vegas in 1970, Elvis explained, "Before I started singing, I was driving a truck and I was working for an electric company. I hauled electrical equipment." And he introduced Gladys and James Tipler, who were in the audience, adding, "Thanks for the job, too!" The previous year, he'd joked to a Vegas audience, "I was just out of high school, and I was studying to be an electrician, and I got wired the wrong way!"

It was Saturday, June 26, and Memphis was sweltering in the heat of a summer's day. Elvis got a call – *at last* – from Sun Studio. Marian Keisker asked if he could get there by 3 o'clock, Elvis later recalled. "I was there by the time she hung up the phone," he used to tell people. With guitar in hand, of course! He'd been called in by Sam Phillips to try out a new ballad called 'Without You'. However, Sam couldn't coax a successful version out of

Right: Elvis and Scotty Moore, 1955

the side-burned young man, so asked him to sing whatever he wanted. Elvis told a newspaperman a couple of years later, "I must have sat there for at least three hours. I sang everything I knew – pop, spirituals, anything I remembered."

And Sam listened, and he heard that *something* in Elvis's voice that made him think it worthwhile to persevere with the young singer. After Elvis had left the studio, Sam got in touch with guitarist Scotty Moore. Moore called Elvis on July 3 and set up an audition. The next day, Elvis went to Scotty's home and ran through his repertoire, as he'd done for Sam. Scotty wasn't too impressed, and neither was another musician, Bill Black, who played doghouse bass in Scotty's band, The Starlight Wranglers. After Elvis had departed, Scotty called Sam and they both decided that they ought to have a tryout in the studio with Elvis.

It was Monday, July 5, and down at 706 Union Avenue, once work was over and the temperature had begun to fall a little, Scotty Moore, Bill Black, and Elvis Presley gathered under Sam's watchful eye, none of them knowing that before the evening was over, something would occur that would change their lives – and indeed, re-shape the sight and sound popular music – forever.

CHAPTER 3
"THAT'S ALRIGHT" ALRIGHT!

It began ordinarily enough; Elvis was still trying out his voice on a couple of ballads. He did 'Harbour Lights' and 'I Love You Because' (complete with whistling introduction and recitation). Sam made recordings of these songs, although there was no special spark to them, just Elvis's young voice, sweet-toned and full of yearning.

They took a break, relaxed and began to fool around, eventually hitting a groove on a tune called 'That's All Right', a 1949 hit on RCA for Arthur "Big Boy" Crudup. They were having fun, makin' music, jamming around. In the control booth, Sam was suddenly alert, listening intently to the impromptu music. He told them to back up and start the song over again. Something instinctively told him that maybe this could be the elusive sound he had been searching for.

What Sam heard and recorded was a completely new type of music, rhythm and blues with a country feel. The guitar and bass underwrote Elvis's clear, uncluttered, and above all, *confident* vocal. That's all right, indeed; what a prophetic title!

'That's All Right' the absolute pivotal, world-changing moment in music

The track was remarkable; besides its fusion of blues and country, it was completely spontaneous. It was pure musical genius, improvisation at its best. What made it even more remarkable was that Elvis barely knew Scotty and Bill. It wasn't as though they had rehearsed and honed the song to perfection. It was one of those happy occurrences when everything was in the right place at the right time. Sam Phillips, who'd often said that he was looking for a white man who sounded black, had found just such a man in Elvis Presley.

No wonder that in October 2003, *Mojo* magazine's readers voted Elvis's first Sun session which had produced 'That's All Right' as the Number One Rock Moment – the absolute, pivotal, world-changing moment in music. Play 'That's All Right' today, and it still sounds as fresh as the day it was recorded.

The musicians returned to Sun, probably the next evening, to cut a B-side, and once again came up with a unique sound. Whereas 'That's All Right' was blues with a country feel, 'Blue Moon Of Kentucky' was country with blues overtones, and Elvis put more drive into this track.

So Sam had his white-boy-who-sounded-black, and he lost no time in getting the disc played on local radio

Left: Sam Phillips at Sun Records. Right: Performing at the Russwood Stadium, Memphis on July 4, 1956

stations. In the first instance, he took the acetate down to WHBQ, where an enthused Dewey Phillips spun it a day or two later. Listening in were Elvis's parents. The shy young singer had taken himself off to the movies. Dewey's listeners liked what they heard and called in requesting repeat plays. Dewey contacted the Presleys, who rushed to the Suzore No 2 theatre, located Elvis, and sent him shaking and scared to death off to the WHBQ studio in the Chisca Hotel. Unknowingly, he did his first interview; Dewey hadn't told him he was live on air! In answer to the DJ's question about which school he'd attended, Elvis mentioned Humes, and only then did listeners realise that he was white.

Below: The Hillbilly Cat with Scotty Moore & Bill Black (EPFC)

Just seven days after 'That's All Right' was recorded, Elvis agreed that Scotty Moore would become his manager, and later in July he was signed up with Sun Records. He played several gigs with Scotty and Bill at Memphis' Bon Air Club before being added to the bill of a big country music show at Overton Park Shell on July 30. Thousands of people flocked to the open-air amphitheatre to see headliner Slim "Rose Marie" Whitman and other popular performers from the Louisiana Hayride. Prior to the show, on July 27 Elvis had given his first press interview to the *Memphis Press-Scimitar*. An advertisement in the newspaper had misspelled his name as *Ellis* Presley.

"WHAT'D I DO?"

When it came time for Elvis to do his two songs – the ones from his first release, Sun 209 – legend has it that it was nerves that caused the leg-shaking that so excited the young females in the audience. As Elvis explained in the 1972 movie, *Elvis On Tour*, "First time I appeared on stage, it scared me to death! I really didn't know what the yelling was about. I didn't realise that my body was moving. It was a natural thing to me. So to the manager backstage I said, 'What'd I do? What'd I do?' He said, 'Well, whatever it was, go back and do it again!'" They encored with 'Blue Moon Of Kentucky'.

'That's All Right' sold well after its mid-July release and several more sessions took place at Sun. On 19 August, a session produced just one track, the haunting 'Blue Moon', with its bluesy vocal drenched in echo. A session sometime in September yielded the next single, 'Good

Rockin' Tonight', coupled with Elvis's unique rendering of 'I Don't Care If The Sun Don't Shine'. Sun 210 wasn't quite as successful as the first release.

Elvis returned to the studio later in 1954 – Sam never kept proper records – and the two tracks recorded formed his third release. Sun 215, issued just after Christmas, comprised the frantic 'Milkcow Blues Boogie' and the smooth, country-styled 'You're A Heartbreaker'. Further sessions, probably in February and March 1955, produced Sun 217, the April release of the lively, hiccuppy 'Baby Let's Play House' coupled with the country-flavoured 'I'm Left, You're Right, She's Gone'.

Just over a year after the first Sun session, Elvis was back at 706 Union Avenue to cut sides which would form his final Sun single. One side of Sun 223, released in August, was 'I Forgot To Remember To Forget', destined to hit the top of *Billboard*'s Country & Western charts the following February. The other side was the sublime 'Mystery Train', which many critics cite as the best track that Elvis cut at Sun. At this July session, Elvis also

recorded 'Tryin' To Get To You', his voice soaring, complemented by Scotty's outstanding guitar solo. This track, plus several others recorded at Sun, was never released by Sam. There was one final session in November, when 'When It Rains It Really Pours' was recorded.

Elvis's Sun tracks are now recognised as pioneering milestones in the history of popular music. They're certainly among the finest songs he ever recorded, timeless gems that retain their vitality year after year, the up tempo tracks still radiating a sense of *joie de vivre* that is all too rarely found in music designed for commercial exploitation.

Above: Sun Records premiere artiste Elvis Presley with Sam Phillips and early manager Bob Neal (Sun Records)

After the Overton Park Show, Elvis, Scotty, and Bill (who wouldn't quit their day jobs until sometime in October), played many times in Memphis, becoming regulars at the Eagle's Nest Club most Friday and Saturday nights. A huge crowd of teenagers watched Elvis perform on a flatbed truck at the opening of a new Katz Drugstore in September.

On October 2, Elvis and the band travelled to Nashville, where Sam had arranged for Elvis to appear on the Grand Ole Opry. His spirited rendering of 'Blue Moon Of Kentucky' in front of an audience that revered its author, Bill Monroe, received only polite applause, and legend has it that the manager told him to go back to driving a truck.

It was getting harder and harder for other acts to follow Elvis on stage.

Two weeks later, on Saturday October 16, Elvis headed south to Shreveport, to sing on KWKH radio's *Louisiana Hayride*, where his unique style was received warmly by the audience. Before his first number, he was interviewed by the emcee Frank Page, who said that he had a new, distinctive style. A recording exists of the introduction, and Elvis's two songs (both sides of his first release). Elvis says, "It's a real honour for us to appear on the *Louisiana Hayride*", and when asked about his style replies, "Well, sir, to be honest with you, we just stumbled upon it". Elvis was a hit with the *Hayride* crowd and three weeks later was given a contract to make regular appearances on the show. He even made a commercial, "You can get 'em piping hot after 4 pm," he sang, "Southern Maid Donuts hit the spot". To date, no recording of this has come to light.

Right: Elvis in New York, July 1, 1956

Elvis and the band began to play gigs at other places, travelling to Arkansas and Texas for country-orientated shows. On December 29, the *Memphis Press-Scimitar* announced that as from January 1, 1955, his new manager would be Bob Neal, the DJ from WMPS radio. Neal got busy booking tour dates for his young protégé.

SIGNS OF THINGS TO COME

Although Elvis's fame was spreading amongst the teenagers, his name was still causing problems. He was billed as *Alvis* Presley on an advertisement for a show in Texas on January 5, 1955. On this show, at San Angelo, he got top billing and hundreds of females rushed the stage. It was a sign of things to come. Elvis already had nicknames, among them "The Hillbilly Cat" and "The Memphis Flash". As a trio, Elvis, Scotty, and Bill were known as "The Blue Moon Boys".

Most of 1955 was spent touring, driving hundreds of miles between gigs all over Texas and most of the Southern states. The venues included many high school gymnasiums, night clubs, theatres, auditoriums, military clubs and American Legion clubs, anywhere where people would gather to watch a country music show. Many of the places were small towns with names like Marianna, Big Creek, Longview, Helena and Breckenridge, although the tours also hit major cities like Lubbock (where legend-to-be Buddy Holly met Elvis), New Orleans, Mobile and Dallas. Sometimes Elvis topped the bill, other times he was billed below more established names like Faron Young, Ferlin Huskey and Hank Snow. When Elvis played Memphis' Ellis Auditorium on February 6 he was billed below Young and Huskey. It was on this date that country music impresario "Colonel" Tom Parker, who had been keeping an eye on Elvis for a while, first met with a (wary) Sam Phillips to discuss the singer's future. Parker began to obtain bookings for Elvis, getting a foot in the door that – for better or worse – would ultimately lead to his taking complete control of Elvis's career.

Press reviews of shows sometimes commented on Elvis's flamboyant wardrobe, describing pink socks, a rust-coloured suit, a black-spotted purple tie on one occasion, and pink trousers and tie with a black jacket on another.

It was getting harder and harder for other acts to follow Elvis on stage. His appeal girls was growing with each appearance, at the same time causing jealousy among their boyfriends. More and more, Elvis began to top the bills, even if his name was still being misspelled on advertisements. He was billed as Elvis "Pressley" for a show at the Eagle's Hall in Houston on March 19. Some live recordings from this date show Elvis in raw, rockin' form on 'Baby Let's Play House' and several other tunes, and during the year a handful of other live recordings were made, including some at the *Hayride* in August. (It's possible that more such recordings will be located and released in the future.) The released tracks all have a raw feel and give listeners a good idea how Elvis handled his early live performances.

On March 23, the Blue Moon Boys and Bob Neal flew to New York to try out for a TV talent show. But Elvis didn't impress the Arthur Godfrey Talent Scouts, so it was back to the high school circuit. The trip to New York was probably Elvis's first flight.

In mid-April, Elvis topped the bill at Dallas' "Big D"

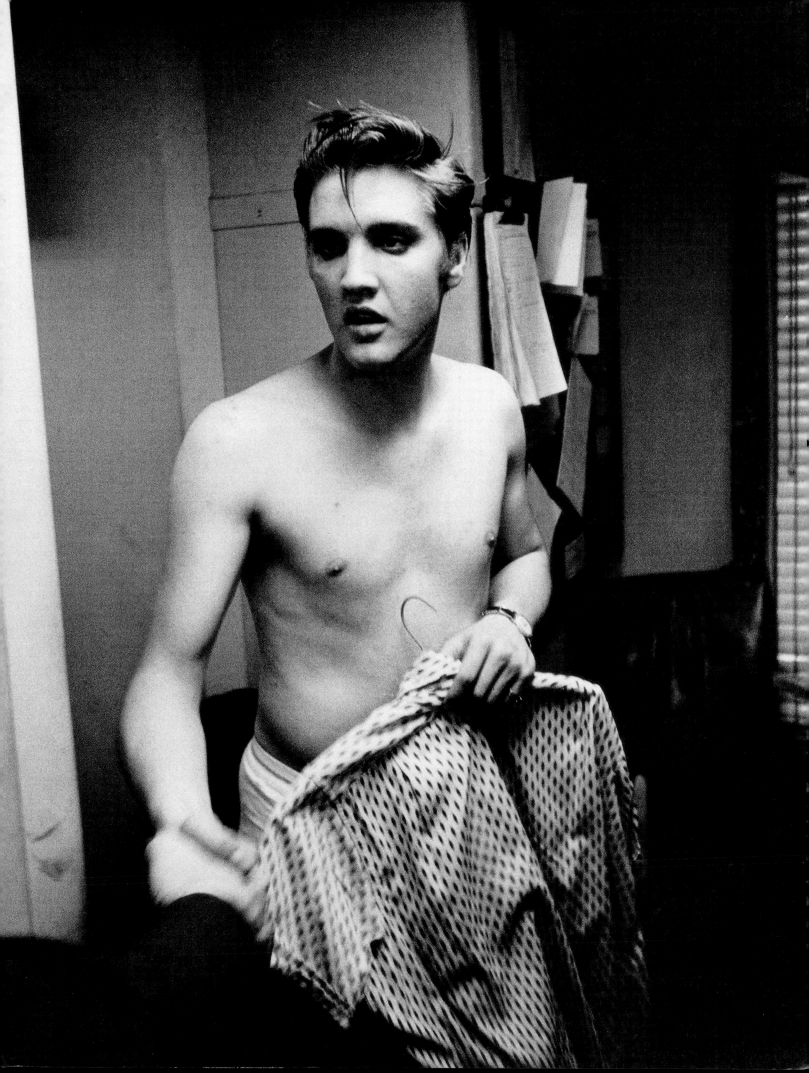

Jamboree, a Saturday night show broadcast live over local radio. Also in April, 5000 people saw Elvis sing at an outside broadcast (known as a "remote") of the Louisiana Hayride in Waco, Texas, and he was a huge hit with the crowd. By May, he was playing dates in Florida. At Orlando, so the story goes, the audience didn't want to see Hank Snow, and left the auditorium when told that Elvis was out back signing autographs! Two days later, in Jacksonville, the 14,000 strong crowd's response to Elvis's comment, "Girls, I'll see y'all backstage" was to riot, with many fans chasing Elvis into his dressing room and proceeding to tear off his clothes. The pink suit ended up in shreds! By now, Colonel Parker knew for certain that Elvis had the potential to be a big star. Conversely, when the tour reached Meridian in Mississippi for the Jimmie Rodgers Festival on May 26, Elvis took part in a street parade, sitting on the bonnet of a Cadillac, and a photo of this shows the crowd taking no notice of him at all.

All the touring meant that Elvis was seeing very little of his home or his parents, and although he called his mother frequently Gladys worried about her son. The family had relocated in the spring of 1955 to 2414 Lamar, and later in the year, would move again to 1414 Getwell.

Elvis needed a new car, too, after his '54 pink Cadillac came to grief while he was headed for Texarkana on June 5. On the 1956 flexi disc, *The Truth About Me*, he recalled, "The first car I ever bought was the most beautiful car I've ever seen. It was second hand, but I parked it outside my hotel the day I got it, and sat up all night just looking at it. And the next day," he ended sadly, "the thing caught fire and burned up on the road." The car was replaced by one that Elvis had recently bought for his parents and he bought a new pink Cadillac a few weeks later.

UP AND COMIN'

Probably Elvis's first-ever poll win came at the beginning of July when he was voted No 1 Up-and-coming Male Vocalist by country music disc jockeys. He made his debut on the national (as opposed to local) charts when on July 16 'Baby Let's Play House' was placed at number 15 in

If you don't have people backing you, people pushin' you, well, you might as well quit

Cashbox's C & W chart. Although Bob Neal was still his manager, as of July 24, Col Parker, who'd been hovering in the background, trying to make deals and entice Elvis away from Sun, would be exclusively representing the young star and looking out for promotional opportunities.

A return to Jacksonville, Florida, on 28 July saw another riotous crowd, and Elvis did an interview with Mae Boren Axton. Among other things, he told Mae, "I have never given myself a name, but a lot of the disc jockeys call me 'Boppin' Hillbilly'." He said that his discs were hottest in West Texas, and asked about the fans in Florida, he said that he wasn't very well known there, adding significantly, he was with a small company and "*my records don't have the distribution that they should have*". He spoke warmly of Scotty and Bill: "I really am lucky to have those two boys, 'cause they're really good. Each one of 'em has an individual style of his own."

Left: Elvis the Hillbilly Cat, 1955

At the end of the interview, he thanked Mae for promoting his records. "You really have done a wonderful job, and I really do appreciate it, because if you don't have people backing you, people pushin' you, well, you might as well quit." Mae Axton would enter the scene again in a few months' time.

Up to this point, Elvis had never had a regular drummer in his band. The Louisiana Hayride's drummer, D. J. Fontana, who'd played occasionally with the Blue Moon Boys, joined them on a permanent basis in early August, and one week later, Col Parker became a "special adviser" to Elvis.

Elvis's taste in clothes seemed to be getting wilder. Bob Luman, who had a huge hit with 'Let's Think About Livin''

in 1960, attended a show in Texas in August, 1955 and described Elvis as wearing red pants and green jacket, with pink shirt and socks! Although the shows and tours that Elvis did were country-themed, and although another of his nicknames was "The King of Western Bop", the Stetson and fringed shirt look wasn't for him. He wore "cat" clothes, and it helped to personalise his image and emphasised the difference between him and other performers.

In September, a new, one-year deal was negotiated by Bob Neal with the *Hayride*, upping Elvis's fee considerably, but carrying a penalty clause should he miss any scheduled performances. Elvis was top of the *Hayride* bill by now, and Sun's rising star, Johnny Cash, was playing on many of Elvis's dates. Bill Haley, who had rocketed to fame with 'Rock Around The Clock', joined Elvis for a show in Oklahoma on October 16. Later in the year, Carl Perkins, another new Sun artist, also toured with Elvis.

Cleveland, Ohio, was the first northern city that Elvis played. He performed on a hillbilly jamboree there in March, and returned in October, when he was filmed on the 20th at the Brooklyn High School auditorium along with Haley and Pat Boone. Local DJ Bill Randle was the subject of the 15-minute film, *A Day In The Life Of A Famous Disc Jockey*, (better known as *The Pied Piper Of Cleveland*). Despite rumours over the years, this movie short still remains unseen. Later the same day, Elvis caused pandemonium at St Michael's Hall in Cleveland after he broke his guitar strings and apparently trashed the instrument.

THE COLONEL STEPS IN

While all this was going on, the Colonel was edging ever closer to having complete control over Elvis. Gladys and Vernon Presley had put their signatures to a document giving Parker the go ahead to get a new recording contract for Elvis. The Colonel telegrammed Sam Phillips to this effect, but neglected to inform Bob Neal.

On November 10, Elvis went to Nashville to attend the 4th annual Country Music DJ convention, telling people that he was going to sign for RCA. He met up with Mae Axton again, who played him a demo of a song she'd co-written with Tommy Durden called 'Heartbreak Hotel'.

Another honour came Elvis's way when he was named "Most Promising Country & Western Artist" in *Billboard's* annual disc jockey poll.

Sam Phillips's asking price for his top artist was $35,000, a huge amount in those days. On November 21, inside Sun Studio, the deal was finalised, with Elvis and his parents present, along with Sam Phillips, Bob Neal, the Colonel, and RCA executives, and Elvis got a $5,000 bonus. The grateful star sent a telegram to Parker next day, which said in part, "I will stick with you through thick and thin". Sam Phillips always maintained that he had no choice but to let Elvis go, so that the young man could fulfil his full potential, and anyway, Sam could put the money to good use in developing his other artists. Since Elvis's success, Sun Records was a magnet for many young hopefuls. As regards Elvis's management contract with Bob Neal, it had a few more months to run.

Above: Bill Haley rocks around the clock with Elvis in Cleveland Ohio on October 20, 1955
Following pages: Performing at the Russwood Stadium, July 4, 1956

Elvis had a photo shoot in New York on December 1, to help the publicity machine along, and RCA re-released all of his Sun singles during the month. The Colonel wasted no time in securing a run of four TV bookings for Elvis on the CBS *Stage Show* at $1,250 a time. An RCA in-house bulletin promoted their new signing as "the most dynamic and sought-after new artist in the country".

Elvis spent Christmas with his parents at his Getwell home and, on New Year's Eve, played the Louisiana Hayride. The new year of 1956 held so much promise.

CHAPTER 4

"SEX SELLS ELVIS IN THE US – HIS MUSIC SELLS HIM EVERYWHERE ELSE"

Elvis celebrated his 21st birthday at home in Memphis, and two days later, travelled to Nashville for his first recording session for his new label. Much was expected of him, and A&R man Steve Sholes needed to justify the large amount of money that his company had spent to sign Elvis.

At the RCA studio at 1525 McGavock Street, Elvis was joined by Scotty, Bill, and D. J. Fontana (doing his first session with Elvis), plus ace country guitarist Chet Atkins, and pianist Floyd Cramer, who'd played with Elvis on some tour dates. Elvis started out by putting plenty of energy into Ray Charles's 'I Got A Woman', a song he'd done on many live shows.

The second most important moment in popular music history, after the session that produced 'That's All Right', might have been when Elvis recorded Mae Axton's 'Heartbreak Hotel', and produced a record that has defied description ever since. It is almost impossible to categorise,

'Heartbreak Hotel' sounds as unusual today as it did almost half a century ago

and is probably nearer to the blues than any other genre. It still sounds as unusual today as it did almost half a century ago. And yet, Sholes wasn't convinced that this was the hit they were looking for.

An evening session later that day, January 10, 1956, produced a rhythm & blues styling of 'Money, Honey', and the next day Elvis recorded two ballads, 'I'm Counting On You' and 'I Was The One'. Backup vocals on this session were taken care of by Gordon Stoker of the Jordanaires, and Ben and Brock Speer. 'I Was The One' was picked as the B-side of Elvis's first release.

On January 25, Elvis flew to New York with Col Parker and checked into the Warwick Hotel, and the band arrived by car two days later. Rehearsals were held for their first *Stage Show* appearance. On the evening of January 28, Elvis stepped live in front of the CBS cameras after an introduction by Bill Randle.

Looking dark-eyed and dangerous, Elvis let rip with a medley of 'Shake, Rattle & Roll' and 'Flip, Flop & Fly'. Hosts Tommy and Jimmy Dorsey and older viewers across the nation probably didn't know what to make of him, and contentious lyrics like, "I'm like a Mississippi bullfrog sittin' on a hollow stump, I got so many women, I don't know which way to jump" must have

Right: Elvis at RCA Studios, New York. July 2, 1956

caused raised eyebrows. But teens all over America recognised something in Elvis that their generation needed after the death of James Dean the previous year. Elvis's second selection was a pumping 'I Got A Woman'. 'Heartbreak Hotel', released just the day before, wasn't sung.

Remaining in New York, Elvis cut tracks at the RCA studios during the next week, including classic interpretations of Carl Perkins's 'Blue Suede Shoes' and Little Richard's 'Tutti Frutti'. Adding greatly to the line-up was pianist Shorty Long, whose boogie-woogie style made 'One-Sided Love Affair' a standout.

The second *Stage Show* took place on February 4, when once again Elvis eschewed singing 'Heartbreak Hotel' in favour of two frantic numbers, 'Baby Let's Play House' and 'Tutti Frutti'. Finally, on the third show on February 11, after a strong performance of 'Blue Suede Shoes', Elvis sang 'Heartbreak Hotel', but it was almost farcical, as the Dorsey Orchestra played an inappropriate big band arrangement. (Thankfully, after this the Dorseys let Elvis and his band perform on their own.) The studio audiences hadn't yet gone overboard about the new singer, and 'Heartbreak Hotel' hadn't yet set the charts alight; a sleeper, it only began to sell well in early March. By this time, Elvis had completed his fourth Dorsey show on February 18, performing

Above: Elvis signs his movie contract with Paramount producer Hal B. Wallis - April 1956 (EPFC)

'Tutti Frutti' again and, for the first time, the emotive ballad, 'I Was The One'.

Elvis was pushing himself too hard, and on February 23 collapsed after a show in Jacksonville. The place seemed to be jinxed as far as he was concerned, with the previous year's riots. At the local hospital, a doctor told him he must slow down. But he was back on stage the next evening, once again exciting Jacksonville's teens.

HITTING THE TOP SPOT

'Heartbreak Hotel' finally entered the charts at an unpromising No 68 on March 3, and it took seven weeks for it to hit the No 1 spot. But once there, it stayed for an amazing eight weeks, and Elvis had his first million-seller.

Meanwhile, the option for two more Dorsey shows had been picked up, at $1,500 a show, and on March 17 Elvis performed 'Blue Suede Shoes' and 'Heartbreak Hotel', undoubtedly giving both his and Carl Perkins's hits a boost. The final *Stage Show* on March 24 saw "Elvis O'Presley" putting a lot of fire into 'Money Honey' and giving 'Heartbreak Hotel' another plug, and by now getting a much more positive response from the studio audience. Watching kinescopes of these shows today, you still get a sense of culture shock. There was the Dorsey Orchestra with its big band era sound; there were hoofers, even xylophone-playing ladies; and then there was Elvis,

looking for all the world like he was from another planet, a vision of the future, in equal doses threatening and thrilling. Everything about him was different – his music, his style, his clothes, his hair. Behind it all was a guy who was having fun, laughing at life, and kicking down music's iron curtain. You notice the outsize microphone and the way Elvis moves, with Scotty's driving guitar, Bill's pumping bass, and DJ's beat underpinning it all.

Above: Andy Griffith, Imogene Coca, TV show host Steve Allen with "Tumbleweed" Presley on the Steve Allen Show *July 1, 1956 (CBS)*

Colonel Parker finally gained complete control of Elvis in March. Bob Neal was out of the picture, and Parker's business associate Hank Snow, who'd assumed he was part of the deal, was also out in the cold. Parker also bought out Elvis's *Louisiana Hayride* contract for $10,000 so as to free him up for more lucrative Saturday night gigs.

Also in March, the Presleys bought a new ranch-style

Everything
about him
different was

house at 1034 Audubon Drive in one of Memphis's nicer suburbs. Vernon and Gladys moved in while Elvis was on tour.

After the final Dorsey show, Elvis flew to the West Coast, arriving on March 25, and spending the next day or so at Paramount Studios in Hollywood doing a screen test for Hal Wallis. The acting part of the test, scenes from *The Rainmaker* opposite veteran actor Frank Faylen, has never been seen, except for a few stills. In 1990, *colour* footage of Elvis lip-syncing to 'Blue Suede Shoes' as part of his screen test turned up on Volume 1 of *The Great Performances* video and caused quite a sensation in the Elvis world. Even back in 1956, screenwriter Allen Weiss recalled, "Electricity bounced off the walls of the sound stage".

Right: Elvis with performers at the Mid South Fair, Memphis. September 23, 1956 (Granlund)

Elvis's first album, *Elvis Presley* (also known as *Rock & Roll No 1*), was released on March 25 and included five Sun tracks that Sam Phillips had never released, plus tracks recorded at RCA New York. It was a huge seller, remaining at No 1 for ten weeks and becoming the biggest selling pop album in RCA's history. It gave Elvis his first gold album. RCA's investment had paid off handsomely – and quickly.

Hal Wallis was so impressed with Elvis's brooding good looks and screen presence that he offered him a non-exclusive seven-picture contract. Elvis put his signature on the dotted line on April 25.

TONE DOWN THE MOVEMENTS

In 1956, Elvis made more TV appearances than in all the other years put together. In San Diego Naval Station on April 3 on NBC's *Milton Berle Show*, he sang and clowned with his host aboard the *USS Hancock*, an aircraft carrier. A second Berle show took place at NBC studios in Los Angeles on June 5, when Elvis's enthusiastic rendering of 'Hound Dog' with its sexy, reduced-pace climax caused a furore in the press and was directly responsible for the way he was presented on *The Steve Allen Show* in New York less than a month later. On the July 1 show, NBC and Allen decreed that Elvis must wear evening dress and tone down his movements. Elvis went along with this, although he wasn't happy. He sang 'I Want You, I Need You, I Love You' in a faux Greek setting, and belted out 'Hound Dog' to a top-hatted basset hound on a pedestal. It was bizarre. On the same show, he took part in good spirit in a "western" sketch with Allen, Andy Griffith, and Imogene Coca.

The next day, at a session at RCA, New York, the fire and feeling that he invested in Leiber and Stoller's 'Hound Dog', doing take after take, may have been inspired by Allen's haughty attitude. The same session, the first where he was backed by the Jordanaires, saw him cut Otis Blackwell's perfect "pop" song, 'Don't Be Cruel'.

At a July 4 show in Memphis, Elvis told the hometown crowd, "Those people in New York aren't going to change me none". Then, in a performance as wild as anything ever seen on an American stage, he showed them what the "real" Elvis Presley would do.

The crowning achievement as far as Elvis's 1956 many TV appearances were concerned was his being signed to three Ed Sullivan *Toast Of The Town* shows for a headline-making $50,000. The first of these took place on September 9 in CBS's LA studios, with portly British actor Charles Laughton in New York deputising for auto-accident victim Sullivan. Elvis sang four songs and said, "This is probably the greatest honour I've ever had in my life". He included both sides of his double-sided smash, 'Hound Dog' (a No 1), and 'Don't Be Cruel' (a No 2). The huge ratings – over 80% of all viewers – justified Elvis's huge fee.

Looking every inch the matinee idol, Elvis did his second Sullivan show in New York on October 28. 'Love Me' was a highlight. Before singing a raucous 'Hound Dog', he joked, "We're gonna do a sad song for you. This song here is one of the saddest songs we've ever heard. It really tells a story, friends. Beautiful lyrics…"

The final *Toast Of The Town* took place on January 6, 1957 in New York, and is memorable for Sullivan and his network's decision to film Elvis only from the waist up. The velvet-shirted, gold lamé waist-coated star still put plenty of spirit into his singing, leaving viewers to imagine what was going on below the belt. During the show, he changed the mood completely when he sang 'Peace In The Valley' with a good deal of sincerity. At the end of the show, Sullivan made some patronising comments that surely must have embarrassed Elvis: "I wanted to say to Elvis Presley and the country that this is a real decent, fine boy… we wanna say that we've never had a pleasanter experience on our show with a big name than we've had with you. You're thoroughly all right."

After the success of 'Heartbreak Hotel', RCA needed another A-side for the next single. Elvis and the band flew to Nashville in April to do a session, but the chartered plane taking them there got lost, and then had a fuel problem, and it was a traumatised group who arrived at the studios on April 14. Only one track was cut, perhaps because of the panic over the plane trip. It was the melodic ballad, 'I Want You, I Need You, I Love You', and became hit number two, reaching No 3 and selling over a million. The gold award for 'Heartbreak Hotel' was presented to Elvis at the session in Nashville in April.

Between September 1-3, Elvis made the first of many visits to Radio Recorders in Hollywood to cut tracks for his second album. It was a productive session, highlights being Leiber and Stoller's emotive ballad, 'Love Me', which, as lead song on the EP, *Elvis, Vol.1*, reached No 6 in the singles charts and sold over a million. Elvis also cut rock'n'roll belters like Little Richard's 'Ready Teddy' and 'Rip It Up', another catchy

"You're thoroughly all right."

Otis Blackwell song, 'Paralysed', and the song from his childhood, 'Old Shep'. When *Elvis* (aka *Rock & Roll No 2*) was released on October, it zoomed to No 1. Another gold album!

Elvis was in demand for live appearances, still playing small venues at the start of 1956 and graduating to huge arenas as Presleymania took hold. The Colonel had had Las Vegas in his sights for some time, and booked Elvis into the New Frontier Hotel for two weeks. He opened in the Venus Room on April 23, but the older audiences failed to appreciate his rock'n'roll songs. Five days later, as 'Heartbreak Hotel' reached No 1 in the charts, he performed a special matinee show for teenagers.

Below: Elvis at the 20th Century Fox commissary with Robert Wagner (to his left) on August 29, 1956. Elvis receives a "Triple Crown" award from Billboard *magazine staff (also seated) for the single "Don't Be Cruel" topping all three sales charts - pop - country and R & B. (Granlund)*

A recording of his final show on May 6 was included on the 1980 box set, *Elvis Aron Presley*. Vegas may not have taken to Elvis, but he took to the city, enjoying the nightclubs and meeting stars like Liberace and Johnnie Ray.

Elvis returned to Tupelo on September 26 and performed to an ecstatic crowd at the Fairgrounds during the Mississippi-Alabama Fair & Dairy Show. No number five place for him this time! Footage exists of the show, with Elvis wearing a velvet shirt and white shoes, and poor quality recordings of the two shows were released on the 1984 box set, *A Golden Celebration*.

Right: When Natalie Wood visited Elvis in 1956, he took her to meet Red Hot & Blue WHBQ radio show host Dewey Phillips at the station's location within the Chisca Hotel, Memphis (Granlund)

A huge crowd of 26,500 people watched Elvis at Dallas Cotton Bowl on October 11. He got almost $18,000 for this show alone. With his huge popularity came the inevitable criticism. Parents, the clergy and the press were on the attack, and Elvis did his best to defend himself and his way of putting across a song. All the headlines and the criticism didn't dent his popularity. Elvis – and Presleymania – was unstoppable. He got a huge welcome when he did a final *Hayride* show on December 15, a "remote" from the Fairgrounds in Shreveport.

Also in December, Elvis dropped by Sun Studio on the 4th of the month and joined in a jam session with Carl

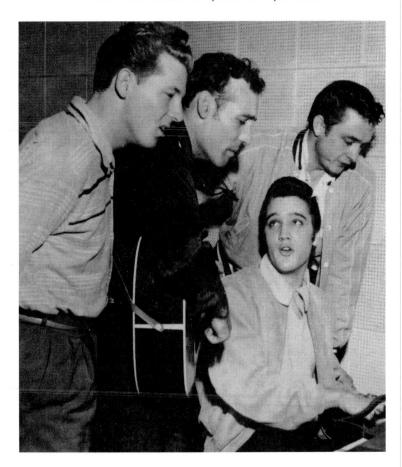

Perkins, Johnny Cash, and new boy, the piano-pumping Jerry Lee Lewis. This became known as "The Million Dollar Quartet", although Cash wasn't featured on the recordings that were released on the album of the same name in 1990.

Elvis enjoyed tremendous success in the United Kingdom, where 'Heartbreak Hotel', 'Blue Suede Shoes', 'Hound Dog' and 'Blue Moon' all made the Top 10 in 1956, but none of Elvis's early TV and radio broadcasts were seen or heard in the UK. So apart from his music and a few teen idol shots that filtered into the British press, the UK was starved of Elvis compared to the US. No one outside of North America had seen a "moving" Elvis Presley, but with Hollywood on the horizon that was about to change.

Although Elvis's screen test had been done for Paramount, it was 20th Century Fox who launched his screen career in their western drama, *The Reno Brothers*, and although the movie only "introduced" Elvis, such was the clamour surrounding his appearance that it became an "Elvis" film. Elvis hadn't wanted to sing in the

Left: The legendary "Million Dollar Quartet" Jerry Lee Lewis, Carl Perkins, and Johnny Cash reunited with Elvis at Sun Studios December 4, 1965 (Singleton / Granlund)

movies but the studio bosses decreed otherwise and four songs were added, three up-tempo, country-flavoured tunes, and one ballad, the simple, heartrending 'Love Me Tender'. This soon became the movie's new title, and gave Elvis another million-selling No 1 hit when released in September. It also became one of Elvis's best known songs, and one most associated with him. He cut the songs on the

Fox Soundstage with studio musicians instead of Scotty and Co. The novice actor did his best to portray Clint Reno, but the best thing about the film was his wild, uninhibited performances of the three up tempo songs.

Elvis's name was linked to many women as his fame grew

Filmed on black and white stock in August and September, with established stars Richard Egan and Debra Paget, it opened in New York on November 15, with a giant cut-out of Elvis dominating the Paramount Theatre's marquee. The teenagers flocked to see it, and it was a huge financial success, although the critics were full of vitriol. Col Parker, coming into his own as the supreme exploitation man, launched EPE – Elvis Presley Enterprises – and peddled merchandise of every description, everything from Elvis Presley lipsticks to statues that glowed in the dark. It sold like the proverbial hot cakes.

Elvis's name was linked to many women as his fame grew, two of the best known being Biloxi fan June Juanico, whom he visited while holidaying on the Gulf Coast in the Summer, and Hollywood star Natalie Wood, who visited him in Memphis in October. Hometown girlfriend Barbara Hearn was seen with him in many photos, too.

As well as the headlines, photographs of Elvis appeared in the press constantly, and the first of an endless line of fanzines devoted to him were published. No photographer came closer to capturing Elvis's meteoric rise to stardom than Alfred Wertheimer, whose evocative images of Elvis, shot mainly in New York and Memphis,

Below: Elvis discusses policy with Colonel Tom Parker on the Love Me Tender *set 1956 (Fox)*

were published in *Elvis '56*, *In The Beginning* in 1979, and have been featured in countless other publications.

The fanzines included *Photoplay's Elvis Presley*, *Elvis Presley Speaks*, *Official Elvis Presley Album*, and *Elvis Answers Back*. This latter magazine had a gold flexi disc attached to the cover, on which Elvis spoke about various topics. Elvis gave dozens of interviews to the press and DJs during the year. Journalists, however, have a way of twisting words around, and the most reliable source of finding out what made Elvis tick comes from audio interviews.

On March 24, while Elvis was in New York for the final *Stage Show* appearance, Robert Carlton Brown spoke to him in his room at The Warwick Hotel. Just a few of the topics discussed were Elvis's first private recording: "We still got the record at home. It's so thin that we can't play it"; his hobbies: "I like motorcycle riding. I like water-skiing"; singers he admired: "I like anybody that's good regardless of what kind of singer they are, whether they're religious, rhythm & blues, hillbilly, or anything else…from Roy Acuff up to Mario Lanza"; his favourite of his own songs: 'I Was The One', and from his first album. 'One-Sided Love Affair'; his thoughts on his fans: "I just

I would never compare myself to James Dean in any way

wish there was some way to go round to every one of 'em and really show that you appreciate their liking you and all"; the Colonel: "He's a very smart man"; his favourite food: "I like pork chops and country ham, cream potatoes, stuff like that"; his clothes: "On stage, I like 'em as flashy as you can get 'em"; on recording: "I have to warm up. I have to get the feeling of what I'm doing"; and movies he had enjoyed: "Recently, I liked *Helen Of Troy*. I liked *The Man With The Golden Arm*. *Picnic* – I liked *Picnic*."

Below: Elvis discusses Love Me Tender script with actress Debra Paget 1956 (Fox)

DJ Jay Thompson caught up with Elvis at a show in Wichita Falls, Texas, in April, and the singer was keen to thank him for promoting his discs. "You really helped me a lot, and I'd like to tell you how much I appreciate it, and all the wonderful people who have been writin' in and buyin' my records, and comin' out to see our shows, because that's really what makes anybody… is the people." He'd voice similar thoughts to many other interviewers.

A DREAM COME TRUE

Another Texas DJ, Charlie Walker, spoke to Elvis in San Antonio in April, when he said of his screen test, "It's a dream come true. It's something I thought would never happen to me… of all people". At an interview in LaCrosse, Wisconsin, in May, Elvis told the (unknown) interviewer about his recent shows in as Vegas. "The first night especially I was absolutely scared stiff. Afterwards, I got a little more relaxed… and I worked harder, and I finally got them on my side a little bit." When Elvis played Little Rock, Arkansas, on May 16, one of interviewer Ray Green's questions was, how did it feel to be a top star? "It feels pretty good," Elvis told him. "It all happened so fast… I'm afraid to wake up, afraid it's liable to be a dream." A rare interview from Los Angeles in early June had Lou Irwin asking about rock'n'roll's detrimental affect on young people (a favourite topic for interviewers). A defensive Elvis told him, "If people are gonna be juvenile delinquents, they're gonna be delinquents if they hear Mother Goose rhymes. Rock'n'roll does not contribute to juvenile delinquency at all."

In July, after his appearance on *The Steve Allen Show*, Elvis did a live telephone interview from his Warwick Hotel room with Hy Gardner, which was shown on split screen TV. Gardner noted that people were predicting that Elvis would be another James Dean. "I would never compare myself in any way to James Dean, because James Dean was a genius at acting," Elvis said. "I guess there's a lot of actors in Hollywood that would like to have the ability that James Dean had. But I would never compare myself to James Dean in any way."

Left: DJ Paul Killinger interviews Elvis just before Elvis' final appearance on the Louisiana Hayride *show on December 15, 1956. (Shreveport Tourist Dept.)*

Along with all the fame came rumours. Elvis turned up unexpectedly at WNOE radio in New Orleans during his visit to the Gulf Coast in early July and told listeners, "I was in Biloxi and I heard on the radio that I was supposed to be engaged to somebody [June Juanico], so I came down here to see who I was supposed to be engaged to!"

While in Florida in early August during the lead up to the first Sullivan show appearance, Elvis gave Paul Wilder an interview for *TV Guide*. Wilder mentioned a scathing press article by Herb Rowe that called Elvis "a no-talent performer", and said his fans were idiots. Elvis's reply to this was, "He ain't nothing but an idiot or he wouldn't sit up there and write all that stuff. He just hates to admit that he's too old to have any more fun." He defended his fans, saying they were "somebody's decent kids, probably, that was raised in a decent home… while they're young, let them have their fun." Most adults, he told Wilder, "are real nice… they don't run people into the ground for having a nice time." He said that he disliked his nickname, "Elvis The Pelvis". "It's one of the most childish expressions I've ever heard."

On *The Truth About Me* flexi disc, done at 20th Century Fox in late August, Elvis revealed, "When I was drivin' a truck, every time a big, shiny car drove by, it started me sort of daydreaming. I always felt that someday, somehow, something would happen to change everything for me, and I'd daydream about how it would be." On the subject of love he said, "I guess I haven't met the girl yet, but I will, and I hope it won't be too long, 'cause I get lonesome sometimes. I get lonesome in the middle of a crowd. But I've got a feelin' that with her, whoever she may be, I won't be lonesome, no matter where I am."

During 1956, Elvis did more interviews than he would ever do again. After this, the Colonel ensured that future access to "his boy" would become far more difficult.

At year's end, Elvis was a millionaire, everybody knew how to spell his name, and his British fan club started functioning from an address in London.

CHAPTER 5
"THE WARDEN THREW A PARTY"

1957 began with a pre-recorded radio spot on which Elvis urged listeners to support the March of Dimes to help polio victims. "The fight against polio is just as tough as it ever was," he said. "They're crippled and the Salk vaccine can't help them to recover. But you can. Remember polio victims. Join the March of Dimes today."

Elvis's latest disc, 'Too Much', recorded the previous September and with a wonderfully improvised solo from

He recorded religious songs imbued with deep sincerity

Scotty, was released on January 4, and although it only reached No 2, still added to his growing number of gold discs.

Eligible for the draft (the US equivalent of National Service), Elvis took his pre-induction physical at Kennedy Veterans Hospital in Memphis, before a quick trip to New York for the final Sullivan show two days later. Directly after the show, he returned home by train, and celebrated his 22nd birthday at the Audubon Drive house.

Ed Sullivan had announced on the show that Elvis was about to go out to Hollywood to start his new movie, naming it as *Running Wild*. This was probably a working title for *Loving You*; *Lonesome Cowboy* was the more common working title. On arrival at Union Station in LA, Elvis checked into the classy Beverly Wilshire Hotel, and prior to starting the movie, cut some of the soundtrack songs at Radio Recorders on January 12 and 13. He also recorded 'All Shook Up', another tune from the pen of the talented Otis Blackwell and his first UK No 1. Perhaps spurred on by the good reception that 'Peace In The Valley' had received on the Sullivan show, he recorded this and two other religious songs and imbued them all with deep sincerity. The balance of the film songs were cut later in January on Paramount's huge scoring stage. This studio, unlike 20th Century Fox, let Elvis use his own musicians, supplemented by a handful of session players, notably pianist Dudley Brooks. Scotty, Bill, and DJ, plus the Jordanaires, would be seen backing Elvis in this movie (and in the two following). At a further session at Radio Recorders on January 19, a fourth religious track was cut. These gospel recordings were destined for a special EP release.

For the film, which would be shot in Technicolour and Vistavision, Elvis had his dark blond hair dyed black. For the rest of his life, with a few notable exceptions, he would continue to dye it.

Right: On Stage with the Jordanaires 1957 (Tunzi)
Left: Elvis with actress Sophia Loren at Paramount 1957 (Granlund)

Elvis's role in *Loving You* was based loosely on his real life rocket ride to stardom, starting off in small towns (and getting the local girls shook up), touring the country, and finally achieving huge fame and attracting controversy, in

this case, rock'n'roll-hating civic authorities. This in many respects mirrored Elvis's own experiences over the past two years.

The character of Deke Rivers, denim-clad and with a special way with a song, suited Elvis well. He looked

It was clear to see that he was gaining in confidence

extremely handsome and he performed his numbers stylishly, from the dramatic 'Lonesome Cowboy' and the rocking 'Got A Lot O' Livin' To Do', to the simple ballad that gave the film its title. He got his first on-screen kiss, from actress Jana Lund. There were still some rough edges to his acting, but it was clear to see that he was gaining in confidence. There was one particularly moving scene set in a graveyard which showed that as a dramatic actor, he had great potential. His co-stars in *Loving You* were Wendell Corey and Lizabeth Scott (playing a kind of

entrepreneurial female Colonel Parker). Pretty newcomer Dolores Hart played Deke's sweetheart. Off-screen, Elvis and Dolores and other young actors enjoyed hanging out and playing and singing together.

Gladys and Vernon Presley made their first trip to the West Coast during the filming. Prior to the trip, Gladys had spent about ten days in Baptist Hospital in Memphis undergoing tests. During a visit to the film set, when the musical finale was being shot, Hal Wallis seated Gladys and Vernon in the audience, and as Elvis rocked and rolled his way down the aisle

Left: Elvis with Brook Benton - one of his favourite singers, backstage in 1957 (Mercury Records)
Below: Elvis with his Loving You co- star Lizabeth Scott posing for a publicity shot on the Paramount lot in a Chrysler Imperial (Paramount)

in 'Got A Lot O' Livin' To Do', Gladys responded by clapping along with great enthusiasm.

As has been mentioned earlier, Elvis never wore "western" clothes on stage. In the movie, however, his wardrobe included some western-styled clothes, and in particular, the red and white outfit worn when he sang 'Teddy Bear'. This scene, backlit in purple, was visually and aurally stunning. Another exciting musical sequence was

Elvis's performance of 'Mean Woman Blues'. The movie was completed by March 10, when the Colonel threw a wrap party on the set and handed out lots of promotional material.

During the filming, Elvis had fitted in another session at Radio Recorders on February 23-24. He finally managed to nail a successful take on 'Loving You', after attempts at previous sessions, and he cut one of his greatest ever tracks, the wonderfully sexy 'One Night'.

GRACELAND

Despite improvements, including a swimming pool and a fence with musical notes on it, the Presley home at

Right: Nudie Cohen, designer of the famous "Gold Leaf" suit with Elvis in 1957 (EPFC)
Far right: Backstage in 1956

Audubon Drive was becoming more and more unsuitable. It was constantly besieged by Presley fans, and the neighbours were none too pleased, as this was a quiet, select area. Another move was on the cards, and on their return to Memphis from Hollywood, his parents found just the place, a two-storey house several miles south of the city that would become legendary. It was, of course, Graceland. It had almost fourteen acres of rolling land, and the house was set well back from Highway 51 South. They called Elvis and told him about it, and a day or so later, he arrived back in town, took a look at the property, and put down a deposit. The deal was completed on March 25, for a total of just over $100,000. Elvis right away got an interior decorator in to modernise the house, which dated from 1939, the land formerly being part of a large farm. Once its Alabama

Elvis's world had changed beyond his wildest dreams

fieldstone front wall was built, and the famous electronic Music Gates, with their guitar-playing figure motif were installed, Graceland would provide the security and seclusion that Elvis was forced more and more to seek as his fame grew to unheard of proportions. Aged just 22, he'd come a long way since moving to Memphis. In the eight-and-a-half-years since he'd left Tupelo, Elvis's world had changed beyond his wildest dreams.

While Graceland was being refurbished, Elvis went out on tour again, and at the first venue, Chicago's International Amphitheatre, had a surprise for the 12,000 fans in the audience – a new outfit, the famous gold-leaf suit. (This stage costume is always referred to as his gold-

lamé suit, but in fact it was leather died yellow with a pure gold-leaf coating). It had been designed by Nudie Cohen of Hollywood and cost a cool $2,500. A frilly shirt and gold tie and shoes completed the outfit. Elvis had the physique to carry off such an over-the-top suit, and it certainly added to the golden boy's stage presence. However, it wasn't the most comfortable of outfits, and after a couple of evenings, he usually wore only the jacket with black slacks. The suit had been Parker's brainchild; Elvis apparently wasn't too keen on it.

When the tour reached Detroit on March 31, Elvis gave a press conference. He was asked about his call-up (after the physical in January, he'd been given an A1 rating) and whether he'd go into Special Services. "I'm not gonna ask for it. If they put me in Special Services, okay. If they don't want to, it's still okay. In other words, just whatever they want me to do, I'll try to do the best I can." He said he wouldn't mind going overseas. Asked about his next film, he said, "My next movie is a prison picture." What was it to be called? Interestingly, he replied, "'The Hard Way'". This would soon change – to *Jailhouse Rock*.

The tour moved on with two dates in Eastern Canada, at Toronto on April 2 (where he wore the complete gold suit again), and Ottawa on April 3, where a local convent school suspended several pupils who'd attended the show.

While in Ottawa, Elvis gave an interview to Mac

was released (backed with a lovely version of 'That's When Your Heartaches Begin', the song that Elvis had cut privately in 1953). It shot to No 1 and stayed in pole position for eight weeks. Apart from giving Elvis yet another gold disc, the phrase "all shook up" entered the language. It also gave Elvis his first UK No 1.

Right: Elvis swings into the famed Jailhouse Rock dance routine

At the end of April, Elvis took the train from Memphis, Hollywood-bound once more. He checked into the Beverly Wilshire and lost no time in starting work at Radio Recorders on the soundtrack for *Jailhouse Rock*. This time songwriters Jerry Leiber and Mike Stoller attended the sessions. They had written the title track, not the easiest song to sing, but Elvis made a superb job of the raucous rocker. Mike and Jerry wrote three of the movie's other songs. The session was interrupted on May 1 when an MGM executive took exception to Elvis's warming up by singing gospel songs, and the star walked out, returning two days later to complete the session.

THE DRAMATIC ROLE HE'D BEEN LOOKING FOR

In *Jailhouse Rock*, Elvis found the dramatic role he'd been looking for; as arrogant Vince Everett, he could play his part with swagger and attitude. Everett was almost an anti-hero. Teamed with Judy Tyler and Mickey Shaughnessy, Elvis brought a lot of rock'n'roll swagger to the role of a man convicted of manslaughter, who on release from prison makes it big in the entertainment world but treats people badly, only to realise the error of his ways in the final reel.

The music fitted the film well. 'Treat Me Nice' and 'Baby I Don't Care' were excitingly performed, but it was the title track that remains perhaps the most memorable of any on screen rock performance ever. It has been called the first pop video, and it certainly helped turn *Jailhouse Rock* into a cult movie. Elvis dislodged a porcelain tooth cap while filming the number, and spent a night in the Cedars of Lebanon Hospital after it was removed from his lung. His famous hairstyle – pompadour and sideburns – was covered with a wig and makeup for the prison scenes.

Filming was completed by June 25, and Elvis headed east to see his new home. Gladys and Vernon had moved in on June 16, and a kidney-shaped swimming pool had been installed. Elvis hadn't been home many days when he heard the tragic news that Judy Tyler had been killed in a head-on car smash on July 3. For this reason, he couldn't watch *Jailhouse Rock*.

Elvis met a new girl, Anita Wood, early in July, and

Lipson, and he was still trying to defend his stage act. "I certainly don't mean to be vulgar or suggestive and I don't think I am… That's just my way of expressing songs. You have to put on a show for people. You can't stand there like a statue." He defended his fans again: "You're not gonna stop a group of young people from having a nice time, because they only grow up once. And they're gonna have a ball while they're growing up. I know I don't blame them and I don't see why anybody else should." Lipson put Elvis on the spot by asking if he thought he'd been successful because of his stage act, or did he really have a good voice "I've never thought I have a good voice," Elvis said modestly. "I just enjoy what I'm doing. I put my heart, soul, and body into it. But I guess one of the reasons people liked it is because it was a little something different."

Above: Actress Yvonne Lime poses with Elvis on the front steps of his recently purchased Memphis Mansion, Graceland, April 19, 1957 (Tunzi)

Elvis's appearances in Canada were the only concerts that he would ever perform outside of the United States. Colonel Parker, branded after Elvis's death amongst other things as an "illegal alien", travelled with his artiste across the border.

About a week before this tour began, 'All Shook Up'

took her, along with his parents, to a private midnight screening of *Loving You* in Memphis. The movie had been premiered earlier that evening, July 10, at Memphis's Strand Theatre. It opened nationwide at the end of July and was a huge box office hit.

The next, short tour was based in the Pacific Northwest and included a show at the Empire Stadium in Vancouver on August 31. Elvis did a press conference before going on stage, answering questions from well-known D J Red Robinson and others, which covered most of the usual subjects. How did he rate himself as an actor? "Pretty bad. I mean, that's something you learn through experience. I think that maybe I might accomplish something at it through the years." Did he mind questions about his personal life? "Anybody that's in the public eye, their life is never private. Everything you do, the public

knows about it, and that's the way it's always been and always will be."

That evening, Elvis put on such a sizzling show for the 26,500 Canadian fans at Empire Stadium that it had to be stopped twice as fans stormed the stage.

Back at Radio Recorders, between September 5 and 7, Elvis laid down tracks for a Christmas album, mixing carols like 'Silent Night' with rock'n'roll-flavoured tracks like 'Blue Christmas' and the great 'Santa Claus Is Back In Town'. This latter was another lyrically clever Leiber-Stoller song, and when Elvis asked the duo for a ballad, they quickly wrote a classic – 'Don't'. This was the last Elvis recording session to feature Scotty Moore, Bill Black and DJ Fontana who resigned over what they considered underpayment.

Right: With actress Venetia Stevenson in 1957 (EPFC)
Left: Scotty Moore (in the shadows on the left) DJ Fontana (drums) and Bill Black (bass guitar) provide the beat for Elvis at the Pan Pacific Auditorium, Los Angeles October 28, 1957 (Tunzi)

There had been no let-up in Elvis's stranglehold of the charts. 'Teddy Bear' reached No 1 after its release in June, and the 10-inch *Loving You* LP hit the top of the album chart. Even the *Peace In The Valley* EP reached No 39 on the singles charts, widening Elvis's appeal and bringing long overdue respect from many adults. Then, in September, came the magnificent 'Jailhouse Rock'. Not only did it reach No 1 in the US, in the UK it was the first disc ever to enter the charts at No 1 when it was issued the following January.

Elvis's dream of a Youth Centre for Tupelo's young people came a step nearer when he did a benefit show at the Tupelo Fairgrounds on September 27. DJ had returned to the fold, and guitarist Hank Garland and bass player Chuck Wiginton completed the line-up. However, the promise of a pay rise lured Scotty and Bill back when Elvis began a

The show attracted negative publicity over Elvis's stage movements

Californian tour four weeks later. A show at LA's Pan Pacific Auditorium on October 28 attracted so much negative publicity over Elvis's stage movements that the police filmed the show there the next evening, but Elvis toned down his gyrations.

Elvis disliked flying and, when he was booked to appear in Hawaii, he went by sea, enjoying a four-day trip on the

USS *Matsonia*, while his band flew to Honolulu. He stayed at the Hawaiian Village Hotel on Waikiki Beach, and on November 10 gave two shows at the Honolulu Stadium and a third show at Schofield Barracks the following day. This was the beginning of a long and happy association with the islands. It was also the end of an era, Elvis's last concert performance of the Fifties.

He sailed back to the mainland on the USS *Lurline* and, after a few days in Las Vegas, returned to Memphis, where on December 20 he collected his call-up papers. At the Colonel's insistence, Elvis asked for a two-month deferment from the Memphis Draft Board so as to give him time to complete his next movie. He made a quick trip to Nashville next day, but didn't perform on the Grand Ole Opry, just waved to the audience. Christmas was spent at Graceland with his folks.

Elvis's Christmas Album was the nation's top seller (it was destined to become a perennial favourite, selling by the million and registering strong sales for many Christmases to come), although its writer Irving Berlin and some DJs didn't care for Elvis's swingy rendition of 'White Christmas'.

Harold Robbins's powerful best-seller, *A Stone For Danny Fisher*, was adapted as Elvis's next Paramount

Street, the Cathedral, a school and Lake Ponchartrain outside the city. Like *Jailhouse Rock*, *King Creole* was filmed in black and white, which added to the sinister atmosphere called for in certain scenes.

ELVIS PRESLEY CAN ACT

Elvis always thought that *King Creole* was the best movie he ever made, and few would disagree. At last, he got the chance to show his acting mettle. Sporting a shorter haircut with cropped sideburns, he turned Danny Fisher into a believable character while the strong supporting cast conjured up the menace of the New Orleans underworld. When the film was released in the summer, it was critically acclaimed. "Elvis Presley can act", the *New York Times* said. Presley fans could be very proud of their idol.

Left: Backstage at the Grand Ole Opry with Little Miss Dynamite Brenda Lee December 21, 1957 (Granlund)
Below: Johnny Cash with his arm around Elvis in Nashville December 1957 (Granlund)

Elvis had fitted in a short session at Radio Recorders on February 1, when one of the songs cut was 'Wear My Ring Around Your Neck', which would be his next single, although it would only reach No 3.

By mid March, Elvis was back home, only a few days away from his army induction. He enjoyed his last few days as a civilian, renting out the Rainbow Rollerdrome nightly. Very early on March 24, he presented himself at the Draft Board in Memphis.

movie, its title changed to *King Creole* to reflect its New Orleans location and its story about a New York prize fighter changed into the struggles of a New Orleans singer. Co-stars were Walter Matthau, Carolyn Jones, Dean Jagger and Vic Morrow, and Dolores Hart again played Elvis's sweetheart. Experienced director Michael Curtiz's brief was to give Elvis respect as an actor.

Left: Elvis with director Michael Curtiz and actor Dean Jagger on location in New Orleans for King Creole 1958 (Fox)

Leiber and Stoller came up with more superb songs, the menacing 'Trouble', 'Steadfast Loyal And True' and the title tune. The excellence was sustained by Wise & Weisman's 'Crawfish', Wayne & Silver's 'Lover Doll' and Tepper & Bennett's bluesy 'New Orleans'. Many fans consider the soundtrack to *King Creole* to be Elvis's best ever. The tracks were cut at Radio Recorders in mid-January, before shooting began on the 20th – by which time Elvis's dramatic ballad 'Don't' was on its way to No 1.

King Creole was the first Presley picture on which he went on location. The cast and crew stayed in New Orleans and locations used included the atmospheric French Quarter with its wrought-iron balconies, historic Bourbon

CHAPTER 6
"OVER SEXED – OVER PAID – AND OVER IN GERMANY"

It was cold in the early morning, but many turned out to see Elvis off, including Vernon and a distraught Gladys Presley, his girlfriend Anita Wood, the Colonel, and plenty of media. After the swearing in, Elvis was put in charge of the other recruits, and they boarded a bus for Fort Chaffee, Arkansas. He was given the number 53 310 761, which every self-respecting fan very soon knew off by heart.

At Fort Chaffee, as the cameras and the press watched, Elvis was kitted out with his uniform and had to pay 65 cents to get his hair cut. When the processing was completed, he was assigned to the 2nd Armoured Division at Fort Hood, Texas (General Patton's "Hell On Wheels" outfit). The new recruits reached Fort Hood on March 29, and the media got their marching orders. The army couldn't stop the endless stream of letters that poured in for Private Presley, though.

On TV, the army sit-com *The Phil Silvers Show* did a spoof featuring "Elvin Pelvin", and novelty records released

He was given the number 53 310 761, which every self-respecting fan very soon knew off by heart

included 'All-American Boy' by Bobby Bare and 'Dear 53 310 761' by The Three Teens. Neither reached the Top 40.

For the next two months, Elvis underwent basic training, which consisted of route marching, KP duty and being shouted at. (And if you ever wondered what "KP" duty stands for it's "Kitchen Police" – peeling potatoes.) It toughened him up and he didn't try to avoid any of the tasks, gaining the respect of his fellow soldiers, some of whom had taunted him on his arrival. He took it on the chin, and was soon accepted as just another soldier –

except, of course, by the fans. They gathered outside the base, hoping to spot him, tried to call him on the phone, and sent him cookies, which he happily shared with his buddies.

At the end of basic training, Elvis was given two week's leave. Col Parker and Anita Wood were there to meet him. Anita had been to Texas on some weekends, and had stayed at the Waco home of Eddie Fadal, who Elvis had met in 1956. During these visits, Elvis had often played piano and sung with Anita.

Right: Vernon Presley admires his son's medals during his first army leave in June 1958 at Graceland, Memphis, Tn. (Planet News / EPFC)

By June 1, Acting Assistant Leader Presley was proudly showing off his sharpshooter and marksman medals to fans at the Graceland gates. He looked tanned and in great shape. He took his parents to see *King Creole*, rented out the Fairgrounds, and went roller-skating.

Wearing his army uniform, he went to Nashville to cut some tracks on June 10, recording five masters, including 'A Fool Such As I', 'I Need Your Love Tonight' and 'I Got Stung' at RCA's new Studio B. The session lasted from 7 pm until 5 am next morning and would be his last for almost two years.

Back at Fort Hood on June 14, Elvis began ten weeks of advanced tank training. He was able to live off base, and brought his parents and grandmother, plus two friends, out to Texas, living first in a trailer and then renting a house in Killeen. Gladys was in poor health and in early August she was taken back to Graceland and then to the Methodist Hospital. Elvis's request for emergency leave wasn't immediately granted, and when he finally flew home, it was to find his mother gravely ill. With Vernon, he stayed at her bedside all the next day, returning home to get some rest. A phone call in the early hours of August 14 brought the tragic news that Gladys had died of a heart attack. She was only 46 and had been diagnosed with hepatitis.

Elvis was devastated. Gladys's casket was brought to Graceland and hundreds gathered outside the Music Gates. For the funeral at Memphis Funeral Home on August 15, the Blackwood Brothers were flown in to sing, and Gladys was buried at Forest Hill Cemetery, about two miles north of Graceland along Highway 51 South.

A MOVING TRIBUTE

A subdued Elvis returned to Fort Hood on August 24, and soon afterwards it was learned that he'd been assigned to the 3rd Armoured Division in Germany, sailing on September 22. He arrived at Brooklyn Army Terminal after a three-day train journey. A press conference was held, parts of which were recorded and released on an EP called *Elvis Sails*. It gave Elvis a chance to praise his fellow soldiers, pay a sincere, moving tribute to his mother, and say goodbye to his fans. About Gladys he said, "Everyone loves their mother, but I was an only child and mother was always right with me all my life. It was like losing a friend, a companion, someone to talk to. I could wake her up any hour of the night if I was worried or troubled about

something, and she'd get up and try to help me." A lighter note was injected when Elvis was asked about his ideal girl. "Female, sir!" he replied.

The USS *Randall* set sail, and during the trans-Atlantic crossing Elvis palled up with Charlie Hodge and took part in a show for the troops, playing piano. Fifteen hundred German fans met Elvis's ship when it docked at Bremerhaven on October 1. With the other troops, he travelled on to Friedburg by train and was billeted at Ray Barracks. He was assigned to Company C as a jeep driver.

Left: Swedish Rock'n'Roll singer Little Gerhard meets Elvis in Germany 1959 (Granlund)

Vernon Presley, Elvis's grandmother and a couple of Memphis friends arrived in Germany on October 4, and checked temporarily into a hotel in Bad Homburg, soon moving to the Park Hotel in Bad Nauheim, a pretty spa town. Elvis was permitted to live off base with them. Before the end of October, they'd moved again, to the Gruenwald Hotel in Bad Nauheim.

Fifteen hundred German fans met Elvis's Ship

The fans back in the USA hadn't forgotten Elvis. The double A-sided release in October of 'One Night'/'I Got Stung' sold 1.5 million.

Before going out on manoeuvres at the beginning of November, Elvis found time to go to a couple of Bill Haley concerts in Frankfurt and Stuttgart. He was also pictured with 16-year-old Margit Buergin, whom he dated a few times.

The manoeuvres took place near the Czech border at Grafenwohr, and lasted for six or seven weeks, during which time Elvis was promoted to Private First Class. He was back in Bad Nauheim in time to spend Christmas Day at the Gruenwald with his family, and his father gave him an electric guitar. Two days later, Elvis went to Frankfurt to see the *Holiday On Ice* show.

Elvis and family moved yet again in early 1959, this time renting out a three-storey house at Goethestrassse 14 in Bad Nauheim, where they stayed for the rest of Elvis's tour of duty.

When Elvis donated blood to the German Red Cross in January, the photo went round the world. Soon after, another photo showed him with a wheelchair-bound boy, as publicity for the March Of Dimes campaign.

There was another visit to the *Holiday On Ice* show in February, followed by a trip to Munich with his buddies in early March to visit Vera Tschechowa, a young actress he'd met during the March Of Dimes promotion. They all went to the Moulin Rouge, where Elvis was photographed with everyone from the showgirls and strippers to the lavatory attendant!

There was another double A-side release in March, 'A Fool Such As I' and 'I Need Your Love Tonight', and the split sales denied Elvis a No 1, just as had happened with the previous release. The first side, with its new, melodic approach, gained Elvis a lot of new fans.

By June of 1959, Elvis had received a promotion to Specialist 4th Class. He was hospitalised in Frankfurt with tonsillitis, and spent his two-week leave, from June 13-27, visiting Vera in Munich again briefly, and then going on to Paris with several friends. They stayed at the swanky Prince de Galles Hotel, strolled down the Champs-Élysées, and enjoyed visiting famous nightclubs like the Lido and the Folies Bergère (and of course, meeting the showgirls!). Elvis gave a press conference at his hotel, and generally enjoyed a taste of his former showbiz lifestyle. In the States, his latest single, 'A Big Hunk O' Love', had restored him to the No 1 spot.

Hal Wallis and a film crew arrived in Germany in August to shoot background location shots for Elvis's first post-army film. Elvis didn't take part in the filming, a stand-in was used.

ENTER PRISCILLA

A significant event took place in September. Priscilla Beaulieu, newly-arrived in Germany with her mother and air force stepfather, was taken to Goethestrasse 14 to meet Elvis. He was immediately attracted to her, and she began to visit him regularly. Other regulars at the house were Charlie Hodge and another buddy, Joe Esposito.

There were more manoeuvres, this time at Wildflecken near the border with Switzerland in October. The same month, Elvis was hospitalised again in Frankfurt with tonsillitis. In December, he began to take twice weekly karate lessons from Jurgen Seydel, beginning a lifelong fascination with the martial art. Although he was still in contact with Anita Wood, Elvis invited Priscilla to his Christmas party at Goethestrasse. Throughout the year, the house had become a Mecca for visiting fans, many of whom got the chance to meet Elvis when he arrived home each day from the barracks.

Another leave in January 1960 saw Elvis and friends off to Paris again, staying at the Prince de Galles and re-visiting favourite nightspots. Jurgen Seydel accompanied Elvis, and took him to meet Japanese karate teacher Tetsuji Murakami. Three days after his return to Friedburg, on January 20, Elvis was promoted to Acting Sergeant. There were more manoeuvres in Grafenwohr in wintry conditions. On his return, he was made a full Sergeant, and put up his stripes. There were only days remaining until his demob.

By this time, RCA had run out of stockpiled material. They had been issuing compilation albums, amongst them, *Elvis's Golden Records Volume 1*, which would be a long-

"I learned a lot, I made a lot of friends"

term seller. Elvis had made some private recordings at home on a tape recorder while in Germany, songs like 'I'm Beginning To Forget You' and 'Earth Angel'. In the States, Colonel Parker had been making plans and negotiating contracts in readiness for Elvis's return to show business.

On March 1, the army held a press conference at Ray Barracks, and the media interest was enormous. Elvis told one interviewer about his army experience: "I learned a lot, I made a lot of friends that I would never have made otherwise, and I've had a lot of good experiences and some bad ones, naturally. It's good to rough it, to put yourself to the test, to see if you can take it."

Right: Elvis with some of his German Fans 1959 (Tunzi)

The next afternoon, Elvis waved goodbye to Priscilla, boarded a military transport plane at Frankfurt, and flew home, stopping off briefly at Prestwick in Scotland, the only time he would ever set foot in the British Isles, where a few lucky fans got to meet him. He arrived at McGuire Air Force Base on March 3, and at nearby Fort Dix, New Jersey, looking relaxed and extremely handsome, and faced another press conference. Asked if he was apprehensive about his comeback, he replied, "Yes, I am. I have my doubts... The only thing I can say is, that I'm gonna try. I'll be in there fighting."

After his final release on March 5, Elvis, with the Colonel at his side, boarded a private railroad car at Washington the next day. The train, the *Tennessean*, was no mystery train. It was taking Elvis home to Memphis.

CHAPTER 7
"A MAN OF THE PEOPLE AND A STAR FOR THE PEOPLE"

On arrival in Memphis on March 7, Elvis greeted the waiting fans and lost no time in going home. Graceland would never be the same now that his mother was gone, but at a press conference that afternoon held in the office building behind the house, he said he had no plans for leaving Memphis. "I'm going to keep Graceland as long as I possibly can," he added. He dismissed rumours about Priscilla: "There was a little girl that I was seeing quite often over there… and she was at the airport when I left, and there were some pictures made of her. But it was no big romance." Asked about future plans, he said, "The first thing that I have to do is to cut some records. And after that I have the television show with Frank Sinatra. And after that I have the picture with Mr Wallis. And then after that, I have two for 20th Century Fox. And after that, heaven knows!"

Before he could start on any of these projects, Elvis had a few days to relax around Graceland and get used to being a civilian again, and see old friends, including Anita Wood. At Gladys's burial site, a beautiful monument had been erected, and a marker placed bearing the inscription, "She was the sunshine of our home". Nearby Burke's Florist had instructions to place a red and white arrangement there every week.

Left: Burke's Law star Gene Barry meets Elvis at the Sahara Hotel in Las Vegas July 1960 (Tunzi)

The *Holiday On Ice* show was playing Memphis in March, and not only did Elvis go and see the show again, he invited the skaters he'd met in Germany back to Graceland. He began to have midnight movie shows at the Memphian, and took his friends, including ex-army buddies Charlie Hodge and Joe Esposito, to the Rainbow Rollerdrome.

It was back to business on March 20. Amid great secrecy, and working from 8 pm until 7 am the next morning, Elvis had a recording session at Studio B in Nashville. Scotty and DJ were there; by this time, Bill Black had his own hit-making Combo. On this and future sessions, players like Hank Garland, Boots Randolph, Floyd Cramer, Buddy Harmon and others would help to create the "Nashville sound".

There was an urgent need for a new single, and the track chosen was 'Stuck On You'. The best track cut at the session, though, was 'A Mess Of Blues'. Working a session with Elvis for the first time was engineer Bill Porter. 'Stuck On You', backed with the ballad 'Fame And Fortune', was released within three days, and it took Elvis back to No 1.

From Nashville, Elvis went on to Miami by private railroad car, greeting fans at stops along the way. He

Graceland would never be the same now that his mother was gone

checked into the Fontainebleu Hotel on Collins Avenue with a small entourage and began rehearsals for Frank Sinatra's *Welcome Home Elvis* show. The actual taping took place on March 26. Elvis wore his army dress uniform for the opening of the show, when he was welcomed by Sinatra, his daughter Nancy, Sammy Davis Junior and Peter Lawford. Changing to a smart tuxedo, Elvis performed both sides of his new disc and sang a duet with Frank on 'Witchcraft' and 'Love Me Tender'.

ELVIS IN PRINT

In 1960, Presley fans could buy their first hardback book, *Operation Elvis*, by newspaperman Alan Levy, and *The Elvis Presley Story* also hit the newsstands.

Tracks for an album were needed, so Elvis returned to Studio B on April 3, and in a really productive overnight session, cut a dozen songs, including 'Fever', 'Such A Night', two fabulous blues, 'Like A Baby' and 'Reconsider Baby', plus two songs that would change his image and sell

Above: In 1960 small screen super star Ed Byrnes who played the part of Kookie in the series 77 Sunset Strip met up with Elvis on the set of GI Blues (Paramount / Granlund)

by the million, 'It's Now Or Never' and 'Are You Lonesome Tonight'. The album, issued soon afterwards, was called *Elvis Is Back*, and it was true in every sense. It was one of his finest albums, yet its sales weren't spectacular.

Hollywood beckoned, and Elvis, hair dyed black again after his army service, took several pals with him on the train, including Charlie Hodge and Joe Esposito, and they took a suite at the Beverly Wilshire.

The movie for which Hal Wallis had done location filming in Germany the previous summer was *G I Blues*. Elvis was at Paramount for rehearsals by April 21, raring to go, and keen to meet his co-star, South African-raised dancer Juliet Prowse, and his new director, Norman Taurog, who'd work on several future Presley films.

The soundtrack was recorded in two sessions – the first at RCA's studio on Sunset Boulevard, and the second at Radio Recorders, where Elvis felt more comfortable. Scotty and D J (plus The Jordanaires, who were on all of Elvis's sessions) were augmented by West Coast session men like Dudley Brooks and Tiny Timbrell. Leiber and Stoller's songs were no longer chosen – the result of a publishing rights deal that they refused to accept – and Elvis wasn't happy with some of the songs he was given. The soundtrack had some good material though, like the sing-along

'Frankfort Special' and the pretty 'Pocketful Of Rainbows', plus a German "oom-pah" song that would become a UK No 1, 'Wooden Heart'.

G I Blues was light-hearted and allowed Elvis to display his comic timing, but the adventures of US soldiers in West Germany didn't bear much resemblance to Elvis's own military service. Much of the comedy was centred around some baby-sitting that Elvis's character, Tulsa McClean, had to do. (Three sets of twins played the baby, Tiger.) Juliet and Elvis made a good on-screen team, and Robert Ivers, as Tulsa's buddy Cooky, was well cast. The German backgrounds added authenticity, and the movie proved to be very popular with cinema audiences on its pre-Christmas release.

On May 12, ABC-TV aired the *Welcome Home Elvis* show, and it got huge ratings, proving that Elvis had lost none of his popularity.

When not on the movie set, Elvis went to several of Hollywood's nightclubs to see performers like Bobby Darin and Sammy Davis Junior, and on several weekends went to Las Vegas to take in more shows by such favourites as Della Reese and Billy Ward. He'd continue to do this through the 1960s movie era.

Shooting and post-production on G I Blues was completed by the end of June, and Elvis went home to Memphis. On July 3, Vernon Presley married divorcee Davada (Dee) Stanley, whom he'd met in Germany, but Elvis boycotted the Huntsville, Alabama wedding. He told a reporter from the *Memphis Press-Scimitar* a day or two later, "I only had one mother, and that's it. There'll never be another. As long as she understands that, we won't have

Elvis Is Back ...was true in every sense

any trouble." He vowed to stand by Vernon, saying, "He's all I got left in the world", and, Elvis being Elvis, he gave Dee's three young sons toys galore.

'It's Now Or Never' was released on July 5 and was a No 1 hit, selling exceptionally well in many countries and gaining gold awards. Once a temporary UK ban due to copyright reasons, was lifted, the disc shot straight in at No 1, staying on top for eight weeks and earning Elvis his first UK gold disc.

Before he left for Hollywood and his next movie, Elvis was awarded his first degree black belt in karate.

Both of Elvis's other two 1960 films were for 20th

Century Fox, and in both the drama outweighed the musical content. The first to be shot was *Flaming Star*, based on Clair Huffaker's fine novel, *Flaming Lance*. As half-breed Pacer Burton, caught between white settlers and Kiowa Indians, Elvis gave a moving performance, and he was ably supported by veterans John McIntire and Dolores Del Rio as his mixed marriage parents. The powerful image of mortally wounded Pacer riding off towards his "Flaming Star of Death" formed the film's final scene, and it was possible to forget that it was Elvis Presley up there on the screen. The film, shot between August and October, included four songs, although two were cut out before it went on general release.

The second Fox film, shot between November 1960 and January 1961, was also adapted from a novel, J R Salamanca's brilliant first book, *The Lost Country*. For the screen, it became *Wild In The Country* and Elvis's role was that of a budding writer, Glenn Tyler, who gets involved with three women and in trouble with the law. Millie Perkins, Tuesday Weld, and Hope Lange played the three very different love interests. Elvis gave a splendid acting performance, singing just a handful of songs. The film was partially shot on location in northern California's wine-growing Napa Valley. These Fox dramas, though, didn't do as well at the box office as *G I Blues* had done.

Above: Frank Sinatra & Elvis rehearse at the Fontainebleu Hotel, Miami Beach, for the Welcome Home Elvis TV show March 1960 (Tunzi)

Elvis became the proud owner of a black Rolls Royce Silver Cloud car in September, the same month that he rented his first LA home. The Beverly Wilshire wasn't keen

Above: Royal Visitors to the GI Blues set on May 10, 1960: King Mahrenda Bir Bikram Shah Deva of Nepal greeted by Elvis. His wife Queen Rajya Lakshmi Shah is seated (Camera Press / EPFC)

on the high-spirited behaviour of Elvis and his entourage. So Elvis and the guys moved to 525 Perugia Way in Bel Air.

Between movies, Elvis was back home in Memphis and travelled to Nashville on October 30 for a recording session at Studio B. In one marathon session between 6.30 pm and 8 am next day, he cut fourteen masters, most of which were destined for his first religious album, the beautiful and sincere *His Hand In Mine*. 'Surrender', the only secular song recorded, followed in the Latin style of 'It's Now Or Never'.

The G I Blues album, released in the autumn, reached No 1, selling extremely well, and 'Are You Lonesome Tonight' was yet another No 1 single, selling over two million after its November release. *His Hand In Mine*, also released in November, got to No 13. The songs varied between hymns like 'In My Father's House' and hand-clapping tunes like 'Working On The Building'. 'Milky

White Way' was undoubtedly included as a tribute to Gladys Presley.

Christmas 1960 was spent at Graceland, and must have brought back memories for Elvis of three Christmases before, when his mother was around to enjoy all the seasonal festivities.

Having returned to Hollywood on January 2, 1961 to finish shooting *Wild In The Country*, Elvis was back in Memphis by the end of the month, but was recalled within days to shoot a new, softer ending to the film.

TIED UP IN MOVIES

On February 25, "Elvis Presley Day" was proclaimed by Governor Buford Ellington of Tennessee and Memphis mayor Henry Loeb. At midday, 225 guests attended a $100-a-plate luncheon at the Claridge Hotel and Elvis received an award from RCA for 75 million record sales. At a press conference afterwards, someone asked why he wasn't on

TV more. "Because of the movie contracts," he replied. "I'm pretty tied up in movies right now and too much television kind of hurts movies a little bit." It had been over three years since Elvis had last done a stage show; was he nervous? "Yes, sir. I don't mind admitting I am. But when I did the Frank Sinatra show in Florida, I wasn't nervous – I was petrified. I was scared stiff!" Asked how many gold discs he had, he answered, "34".

Later that day, Elvis gave his first stage shows since late

In the early Sixties, there was a wonderful pureness to Elvis's voice

1957 at Ellis Auditorium, backed by Scotty, DJ, Floyd Cramer, Boots Randolph and The Jordanaires, plus the Larry Owens Orchestra. There was a matinee and an evening show. Elvis, in white tuxedo and black trousers, performed titles like 'Heartbreak Hotel', 'Love Me', 'A Fool

Such As I', 'One Night', 'Doin' The Best I Can', and more, and his latest hit, 'Surrender', and closed with 'Hound Dog'. A great many Memphis charities, along with the Elvis Youth Centre in Tupelo, benefited from the $51,612 raised.

Above: Princesses Margrethe of Denmark, and Astrid of Norway, and Margaretha of Sweden meet Elvis on the set of GI Blues, *June 4, 1960 (Tunzi/EPFC)*

Driving his Rolls Royce, Elvis went to Nashville on March 8 and in a rare public appearance addressed the Tennessee State Legislature and accepted a framed certificate from Governor Ellington making him an honorary Colonel. In his acceptance speech, he said it was one of the greatest honours he'd ever had in his entire career, and vowed never to leave Tennessee for Hollywood.

In the early Sixties, there was a wonderful pureness to Elvis's voice, and a recording session at Studio B on March 12 showcased this to perfection in numbers like 'Gently', 'It's A Sin' and 'Starting Today'. This latter song was written by Don Robertson, and Floyd Cramer copied Don's

Above: Steve Forrest, Barbara Eden and Elvis on the set of Flaming Star *1960. (FOX)*

unique "slip-note" piano style on this and other Robertson compositions that Elvis recorded. There were some terrific up tempo numbers cut at the session, too, notably 'Judy' and 'I'm Comin' Home'. The session provided material for the *Something For Everybody* album, which would hit No 1 in the summer.

Only days after this session, Elvis was out in Hollywood cutting songs for his next Paramount movie, *Blue Hawaii*. Of necessity, the soundtrack had a Hawaiian flavour, with lovely melodies like 'Aloha Oe', 'Hawaiian Wedding Song', 'No More' and the title track. The most significant song recorded was the ballad 'Can't Help Falling In Love'.

On March 25, Elvis flew via Pam-Am to Honolulu (telling media at the airport that he was going to take all the leis off his neck so that he could walk!), and gave a press conference at the Hawaiian Village Hotel for both media and local high school reporters, and accepted more awards. That evening, 6,000 fans watched Elvis on stage at Bloch Arena. The gold-leaf jacket had been brought out of mothballs. On what would be his last live appearance for over eight years, Elvis did fifteen songs, including 'Reconsider Baby' and 'Swing Down Sweet Chariot', and many of his big hits. The show, another benefit, raised over $62,000 for the USS *Arizona* memorial at Pearl Harbour.

ELVIS: HERO OR HEEL

Back in 1957, a fanzine called, *Elvis Presley, Hero or Heel* had been published. By 1961, few people would have dared to call Elvis a heel after his charitable efforts, not to mention his exemplary army record.

Two days after the benefit show, shooting began on *Blue Hawaii*. The main co-stars were Joan Blackman as Elvis's Hawaiian sweetheart, and London-born Angela Lansbury, as his mother, who was actually only nine years older than Elvis! In his role of

Right: Choreographer Charlie O'Curran (who was at one time married to Gladys Presley's favourite singer Patti Page) is seen here with Elvis on the set of Blue Hawaii *(EPFC)*

Right: Boxer Rocky Graziano (right) meets Elvis on the Paramount set for Blue Hawaii in 1961 (Granlund)
Left: "The first thing I'm going to do is take these leis off my neck so that I can walk!" jokes Elvis when he arrives at Honolulu Airport on March 25, 1961 (Tunzi)

tourist guide Chad Gates, Elvis played out a light-hearted story that showed off the scenic beauty of Oahu and Kauai, and he looked and sounded good; too good, really. Such was the outstanding box-office success of *Blue Hawaii* that it set an unfortunate template for many of the movies that followed.

While making the film, Elvis discovered the romantic resort of Coco Palms Hotel on Kauai. Several scenes were filmed there, including the colourful 'Hawaiian Wedding Song' finale, and it was a place to which he'd return on vacation in the future.

He looked and sounded too good, good, really

Once the film was completed, Elvis returned to Tennessee. At Studio B on June 25, he cut several songs,

amongst them 'His Latest Flame' and 'Little Sister', both penned by Doc Pomus and Mort Shuman, who would write many fine songs for Elvis. A week later, at the same studio, he cut the soundtrack for his next movie, *Follow That Dream*. They included a pretty ballad, 'Angel', written by another prolific team, Sid Tepper and Roy Bennett.

Follow That Dream was shot on location in Florida in the summer for United Artists. Elvis benefited from the talents of character actor Arthur O'Connell, while the

Below: During a break in shooting Follow That Dream in Florida Elvis & Red West demonstrate their karate skills. West plays a security guard in the movie (Tunzi)

65

Left: British DJ Jimmy Savile meets his idol Elvis Presley for the first time in 1961 on sound stage 4 at Fox Studios during the filming of Wild In The Country, *presenting Elvis with a gold disc for the British million selling single 'It's Now or Never' (Sir Jimmy Savile OBE KCSG)*

Below and right: Bobby Darin joins up with Elvis in Las Vegas for the opening night of the George Burns show at the Sahara Hotel & Casino July 1960 (Granlund)

Above: Brenda Lee visits Elvis Presley on the set of Wild In The Country *1961 (Fox / Granlund)*

Top right: Pat Boone visits Elvis on the Wild In The Country *movie set back in 1960 (Granlund)*

female lead was Anne Helm. In his role as none-too-bright Toby Kwimper, Elvis was able to demonstrate both his comedic and dramatic skills. The film, one of Elvis's finest, was adapted from Richard Powell's hilarious novel, *Pioneer Go Home*, about a family of homesteaders coming up against Government small-mindedness and winning the day. The few songs were incidental to the plot and Elvis's hair was left its natural colour in this film.

The film was completed in Hollywood by August, and Elvis spent the next few weeks commuting between Memphis and Las Vegas. 'His Latest Flame' and 'Little Sister' was released in August but split sales prevented a No 1. The *Blue Hawaii* soundtrack album came out in October and topped the album charts, enjoying massive, long-term sales. A session at Studio B on October 5 was notable for an exquisite Don Robertson ballad, 'I Met Her

Above: Elvis Monthly *Editor Albert Hand makes a presentation to Elvis on the set of* Kid Galahad *1961 (EPFC) Left: Elvis & Colonel Parker on the film set of* Follow That Dream *(Warner/MGM)*

Today', and a catchy, future hit, 'Good Luck Charm'. Then it was off to Hollywood again where, along with his regular entourage, Elvis was accompanied by his new pet, a mischievous chimpanzee called Scatter.

He was **more** than a mere rock'n'roll singer

The boxing movie, *Kid Galahad*, based on a novel by Francis Wallace, was Elvis's second movie for United Artists. His hair was again left its natural colour. Joan Blackman co-starred again, along with Gig Young, Charles Bronson and Lola Albright. The movie had a handful of songs, but was of a dramatic nature and Elvis put in a very credible performance as a reluctant boxer with a lethal knockout punch. Some scenes were filmed against a backdrop of autumn colour in Idyllwild, California, where Elvis had to face some pretty chilly weather.

After he returned to the comfort of the Hollywood studios, on November 21 he changed addresses, temporarily leaving the Perugia Way house and moving into another rented home at 10539 Bellagio Road, Bel Air.

Blue Hawaii was in cinemas before the end of November, and proved to be a huge success, while a new single, 'Can't Help Falling In Love' just missed the No 1 slot in the USA. In the UK, Elvis was having an unprecedented run of No 1s in the early Sixties: ten chart-toppers between November 1960 and July 1963.

Kid Galahad shooting was completed before Christmas, but Elvis didn't return to Graceland, where Vernon and his new wife and her three boys were living. Instead, he went to Las Vegas and spent Christmas at the Sahara Hotel. Before the end of December, Vernon moved to a new home at Hermitage Drive, not far from Graceland.

1961 was one of Elvis's most successful years; he had consolidated his fame and had a huge following. He had proved that he could adapt his style; he was more than a mere rock'n'roll singer.

The bubble was about to burst, though…

Above: Elvis Monthly Editor Albert Hand makes a presentation to Elvis on the set of Kid Galahad 1961 (EPFC) Left: Britain's Billy Fury presents silver disc awards to Elvis on the set of Girls! Girls! Girls!, 1962

For the next few years, Elvis was locked into movie after movie, with no personal or TV appearances and very few non-soundtrack recording sessions. With few exceptions the movie scripts didn't do his talent (or his reputation) justice, and the film songs he was obliged to record were often very weak. He became disillusioned, and though he never allowed his feelings to show in public, he complained of his frustration in private to his inner circle. Much of the fault lay with Colonel Parker and the Hollywood producers, all of whom seemed interested only in how much income Elvis could generate for them. Culture was never as bankable as processed schlock.

The first signs of the decline in standards occurred in 1962. The first of the two movies made that year was

Culture was never as bankable as processed schlock

Paramount's *Girls! Girls! Girls!*, and while it was still reasonably entertaining, with a decent soundtrack highlighted by 'Return To Sender', it had all the hallmarks of a "formula" film. Location scenes were shot in Hawaii in April, on Oahu and the Big Island, and Elvis looked lean and handsome as fishing boat skipper Ross Carpenter. Stella Stevens and Laurel Goodwin vied for his on-screen affections. The soundtrack was cut at Radio Recorders in late March, and the film was completed by mid May.

In late August Elvis was back in Tinseltown for his next movie for MGM, his first for the studio since 1957's legendary *Jailhouse Rock*, which was greeted by the first murmurings of real discontent from Presley fans. *It Happened At The World's Fair* was shot partly on location at the 1962 Seattle World's Fair and co-starred Joan O'Brien and Gary Lockwood, and (depending on your point of view) young Vicky Tiu as a little cutie/little horror.

Children would become a feature of several Elvis pictures, not always to artistic advantage. The backgrounds of the World's Fair gave the film some credibility, but the soundtrack's quality had taken a dip. There was a torchy song, 'Relax', sung to great effect as Mike Edwards (Elvis) tried to seduce his date, but little else of quality.

There was only one non-soundtrack session in 1962. On March 18-19, Elvis laid down tracks at Studio B, the bulk of which were destined for the *Pot Luck* album released in June. 'Something Blue' was a standout track, Floyd Cramer's tinkling piano adding a special touch. A Latin-styled song called 'You'll Be Gone' bore the song writing credits, West/Presley/Hodge. Red West had been a friend since schooldays in Memphis, and was part of Elvis's entourage, as was Charlie Hodge. Collectively, the entourage was known as the "Memphis Mafia".

'Good Luck Charm' gave Elvis a No 1 in the spring, 'She's Not You' peaked at No 5 in the summer, and 'Return To Sender' made it to No 2 in the autumn, selling well over a million. The *Pot Luck* and *Girls! Girls! Girls!* albums reached No 4 and No 3 respectively. Elvis was still selling a lot of records.

Between movies, Elvis spent plenty of time in Las Vegas watching his favourite performers, and in Memphis enjoying midnight movie shows and late nights out at the Fairgrounds with his friends and the fans who were lucky enough to be invited along. He had his own 16mm movie projector in the basement TV room at Graceland, too. Still not keen on flying, he bought a Dodge motor home for the trips between Memphis and California, and had it customised in Hollywood by Kustom King George Barris.

Elvis had always enjoyed playing American football. Having been turned down by the Humes High School Tigers during his schooldays, he set up a team of his own in the early Sixties, and while in LA his side would play on

Left: A very young Kurt Russell kicks Elvis in a scene from It Happened At The World's Fair *1962 (MGM / Granlund)*

Sundays against a team of stars like Ricky Nelson and Pat Boone at De Neve Park near his home.

In June 1962, Elvis talked Priscilla Beaulieu's parents into letting her visit the USA for two weeks. She flew to LA from Germany, and two days later Elvis took her and some of his entourage to Las Vegas, where they stayed at the Sahara. Elvis was still involved with Anita Wood, but in early August Anita announced that she and Elvis had split up. Priscilla returned to the States to spend Christmas with Elvis.

During the shooting of *It Happened At The World's Fair*, Elvis gave a rare in-depth interview to Lloyd Shearer, telling the journalist that he was proud of the way he'd been brought up to treat people with respect and consider their feelings, how he'd hoped to go to college, that he never thought of himself as a ladykiller, and how he hoped to improve in a lot of ways, particularly acting. "I've experienced a lot of the different phases in life. I've experienced happiness and loneliness, and the wealthy side of life, the average side of life, not having anything… And tragedy, like losing my mother while I was in the army. I think that things like that, as tragic as they are, tend to make you a little better human being, 'cause you learn more about yourself. It gives you a better understanding of yourself as well as other people." Portions of this insightful interview were included on the 1980 box set *Elvis Aron Presley* in monologue form.

THE MOVIE MACHINE ROLLS ON

The movie machine rolled on in 1963. There was *Fun In Acapulco* for Paramount, and *Viva Las Vegas* and *Kissin' Cousins* for MGM. *Fun In Acapulco* was another "formula" movie with lots of colour and agreeable scenery (although Elvis didn't go to Mexico for any location filming). Bond girl Ursula Andress co-starred, and what lifted the film was its sparkling, Latin-styled soundtrack. Elvis found the right mood on numbers like 'El Toro' and 'Guadalajara', and 'Mexico' was very catchy. He played Mike Windgren, a former trapeze artist trying to overcome his fear of heights; cue a spectacular 136 foot dive off La Quebrada (not by Elvis himself, of course).

With the casting of vivacious Ann-Margret as Elvis's co-star, and locations in and around the gambling city, *Viva Las Vegas* saw a marked improvement. Elvis and Ann made a charismatic pair as Lucky (Jackson) and Rusty (Martin), and became close off-screen, too. Elvis played a race-car driver, and the songs were well filmed, especially the duet, 'The Lady Loves Me' and the punchy title track. It was one of Elvis's best and most popular musicals, and it was a pity that Elvis and Ann weren't teamed up again on screen.

Unfortunately *Kissin' Cousins* was a very different kettle of fish. The low budget and short filming schedule was all too obvious, despite some location filming in picturesque Big Bear, California, standing in for the Smokey Mountains of Tennessee. It was unusual to see Elvis playing both dark-haired air force officer Josh

Elvis and Ann made a charismatic pair ... and became close off-screen

Morgan, and (in a blond wig) his hillbilly cousin Jody Tatum. Arthur O'Connell did his best as a moonshiner opposed to leasing his land to the Government, but the script was weak and the mostly poor songs fitted awkwardly into the film. And yet, on release, the film was very popular in the USA.

Elvis had just one non-soundtrack session in Nashville in 1963. Between May 26 and 27, he cut over a dozen tracks, several of which ended up as bonus songs on soundtrack albums. 'Devil In Disguise' was chosen as an A-side, and gave Elvis his biggest hit of the year, peaking at No 3 in the US. His records were still selling well, mostly reaching the top 10, but the days of automatic chart toppers were over.

Elvis moved back to 525 Perugia Way in January, 1963, and Priscilla moved to the USA in March, supposedly to live with Elvis's father and stepmother while completing her final year at Immaculate Conception High School in Memphis. She graduated in May and, when he was home, joined in Elvis's midnight

Right: Ann Margret and Elvis on the set of Viva Las Vegas *1963 (MGM)*

movie shows and parties, only going out to Hollywood in November after stories in the press linked Elvis with Ann-Margret. It seemed Elvis was torn between the two women, but after Ann told the London press that she was in love with Elvis, their relationship cooled, although they always remained close friends. It was Priscilla who spent Christmas at Graceland with Elvis.

During 1964, while Elvis was chained to the Hollywood studios, The Beatles were conquering America.

Elvis and the Colonel graciously wished them well, sending a telegram on the occasion of their February 9 appearance on the Ed Sullivan Show.

Elvis made a rare personal appearance at Long Beach, California, on February 14 to present Roosevelt's former presidential yacht, the USS *Potomac*, to entertainer Danny Thomas to benefit St Jude's Children's Research Hospital in Memphis. Elvis had bought the yacht for $55,000 at an auction, and had initially offered it to the March Of Dimes. Most of the many charitable donations that Elvis made got little or no publicity, and that was the way he wanted it.

Below: Elvis Memphis Mafia buddies join Elvis and Jim Brown (Cleveland Browns Football Club) on the Paramount lot during the filming for Roustabout (left to right: Billy Smith, Alan Fortas, Richard Davis, Jim Brown, Elvis, Joe Esposito, Marty Lacker and Jimmy Kingsley in 1964 (Paramount / Granlund)

Roustabout was the year's first movie, made at Paramount and on location in California. The story of a travelling carnival, it cast Elvis as Charlie Rogers, a singer turned roustabout, and co-starred veteran actress Barbara Stanwyck. Charlie had attitude, giving Elvis a chance to act mean. The soundtrack had one or two decent songs, the best of which was Leiber and Stoller's 'Little Egypt', a hit for The Coasters.

Girl Happy for MGM came next on Elvis's Hollywood roller coaster, and cast Shelley Fabares in the first of her three co-starring roles with Elvis. The action took place at Fort Lauderdale, Florida, when singer Rusty Wells (Elvis) entertained vacationing students while secretly chaperoning Valerie (Shelley). The film had its moments, such as Elvis breaking *into* jail and emerging dressed in drag. The pretty ballad, 'Puppet On A String', was amongst the better songs on the soundtrack. Yet the decidedly poor 'Do The Clam' was chosen as A-side of a new single.

Right: In the spring of 1964 Jimmy Savile returns to America to discuss with Colonel Parker a British idea by Todd Slaughter to present Elvis live on television by satellite in a programme hosted by Redifussion TV called Elvis via Telstar, *seen here on the Paramount set with the King during a break the in filming for the movie* Roustabout. *(Sir Jimmy Savile OBE KCSG)*

There weren't any new songs in the next movie, *Tickle Me*. Allied Artists Studio was in financial trouble, so to cut costs previously released songs were used. It gave fans a chance to see Elvis doing the bluesy 'It Feels So Right' and belting out 'Dirty Dirty Feeling'. The staging of some songs left much to be desired, and there were several obvious technical errors in the film, in which Elvis played rodeo

champion turned dude ranch hand Lonnie Beale. There were some very funny scenes set in a western ghost town, but little else to recommend this film, which co-starred Jocelyn Lane and Julie Adams.

SPIRITUAL LEANINGS

During 1964 Elvis became interested in spiritual books like *The Impersonal Life* which was recommended to him by Larry Geller, his hairdresser. Geller's influence on Elvis caused rifts in the entourage, and his presence was not looked upon kindly by Col Parker. That year, too, Elvis was appointed a "Special Deputy Sheriff" in Memphis, while Vernon, Dee and her sons moved into a new house at 1266 Dolan, which had access to the rear of Graceland.

The best non-film song that Elvis recorded in 1964 (at a short session in Nashville in January), was 'It Hurts Me' which ended up as the B-side to 'Kissin' Cousins'. The hits

were getting harder to come by, as singles began to miss the Top 10. The *Roustabout* album, however, reached No 1 in the first week of January, 1965, a special gift for Elvis on his 30th birthday.

It's hard to find anything positive to say about Elvis's thirtieth year. While all around him pop music was experiencing its most creative phase since he burst on the scene a decade earlier, with The Beatles, Bob Dylan and The Rolling Stones spearheading a new cultural renaissance amongst teenagers, Elvis made three films, none of which had much going for them. Many people cite *Harem Scarem* (MGM) as Elvis's worst movie ever. Badly made, with our hero as singing karate expert Johnny Tryonne trying to avoid assassinating a Middle Eastern king, and falling for his daughter (Mary Ann Mobley), it is best regarded as a spoof. Elvis didn't look comfortable in his Eastern

Above: Chatting to producer Hal B. Wallis on the Roustabout *set 1964 (EPFC)*

Left: French singing star Mireille Mathieu meets Elvis on the Spinout *film set 1966 (Jean-Marie Pouzenc)*

Left: Barbara Stanwick visits Elvis on the set of Frankie & Johnny in 1965 (Granlund) Right: Elvis is visited by football player turned actor Jim Brown on the Roustabout Paramount film set (Tunzi)

costumes, and the songs were pretty poor.

United Artist's *Frankie And Johnny* was only slightly better. The singing title characters were played by Elvis and pretty Donna Douglas, who'd charmed TV viewers in *The Beverly Hillbillies*. The setting was a Mississippi riverboat, and on the credit side, the costumes were colourful and there was a marvellous sequence built around the title song. The soundtrack had a certain merit; Elvis performed the songs well, and these included a welcome blues, 'Hard Luck'. The script let the film down; it was played for comic effect, whereas, as a drama, it would have had far more impact.

Paradise, Hawaiian Style, for Paramount, promised much and proved to be a disappointment for many. *Blue Hawaii* it wasn't – apart from some stunning scenery. Shot on location in the islands, and featuring scenes at the Polynesian Cultural Centre at Laie, Oahu, it was more or less a travelogue. British actress Susanna Leigh played opposite Elvis, in his role as helicopter charter pilot Rick Richards. The soundtrack included embarrassingly poor songs like 'Queenie Wahine's Papaya' and 'A Dog's Life'. No wonder Elvis laughed his way through take after take at the recording session. There was one standout song, 'Drums Of The Island', featuring performers from various Polynesian cultures along with Elvis.

The surprise hit of the year (No 3 in the US and No 1 in the UK) was a track left over from the *His Hand In Mine* session in 1960, 'Crying In The Chapel'. Generally, singles

were under-achieving, yet soundtrack albums still dented the Top 10.

Maybe as an antidote to his declining interest in his Hollywood movies, Elvis began to visit the Self-Realisation Lake Shrine in Pacific Palisades, California, where he continued his spiritual search. The shrine prompted Elvis to have a Meditation Garden built at Graceland, and work on this was completed by the end of the year.

No doubt Elvis was very moved when in August he went to see the simple white memorial built over the sunken hulk of the USS *Arizona* at Pearl Harbour in Hawaii. Thanks to his 1961 benefit show, the memorial had been completed.

There were big headlines in late August when Elvis and The Beatles met at his Perugia Way house on August 27. They swapped stories and jammed late into the night as fans who'd found out about the "secret" meeting crowded round Elvis's fence and gates. Beatles manager Brian Epstein and Colonel Parker stood together at the side and watched the meeting.

On a sad note, Bill Black died of a brain tumour on October 21, aged only 39. Elvis wasn't able to attend the funeral for fear of causing a commotion, but expressed his sadness, saying, "I can hardly explain how much I loved Bill".

A new year, a new house: when Elvis arrived in Hollywood in early February, 1966, he moved into a new

Elvis and The Beatles swapped stories and jammed late into the night

rented house at 10550 Rocca Place, Bel Air, which hopefully would provide more privacy for Elvis, Priscilla, and the ever-present entourage. He also had a new Greyhound bus being customised by George Barris.

Film number 23 was *Spinout* for MGM. Elvis was cast as Mike McCoy in a typical musical – a car-racing, girl-chasing adventure that had lots of pace. On the soundtrack, 'Am I Ready' was one of the sweetest ballads he'd ever sung, while 'Never Say Yes' and 'I'll Be Back' were catchy, up-tempo songs. The likeable Shelley Fabares co-starred.

The film completed, Elvis left Hollywood behind as he drove his new Greyhound bus Memphiswards. Between his next scheduled films, a recording session would take place that would signal a renewed interest in his career.

CHAPTER 9
"GOODBYE HOLLYWOOD – HELLO WORLD"

On May 25, Elvis arrived at Studio B in Nashville and met his new record producer, Felton Jarvis. The main aim of the session, which lasted until the 28th, was to cut a second religious album, something very dear to Elvis's heart. As well as The Jordanaires, a second gospel group, The Imperials, was in the studio. One of their members was Jake Hess, whom Elvis idolised.

Elvis's love of sacred music shone through on every track he cut. There were fast-paced hand-clappers – 'Run On', 'So High', 'By And By', and 'If The Lord Wasn't Walking By My Side'. There were slower numbers – 'In The Garden', 'Where No-one Stands Alone', 'Stand By Me',

'Farther Along', and the finger-snapping 'Where Could I Go But To The Lord'. And there was the hymn that gave the album its title, 'How Great Thou Art', Elvis's favourite gospel song. He sang it, as he did all the rest, with conviction and sincerity. No wonder that *How Great Thou Art* was picked as "Best Sacred Performance", giving Elvis the first of his three Grammy awards for gospel recordings in 1967.

Several secular songs were cut at the session, among them Boy Dylan's 'Tomorrow Is A Long Time', which the songwriter subsequently declared to be one of the best

Right: Elvis with Colonel Parker and Larry Geller clowning on the set of Double Trouble *(Tunzi)*
Below: British actress Annette Day co-stars with Elvis in Double Trouble *(MGM)*

Above: Elvis accepts a Youth Leadership Award on the set of Easy Come Easy Go (EPFC)

versions of any of his songs. He was right, it was superb! 'Down In The Alley' was also very good; Elvis always had a special feeling for bluesy tunes. Both songs ended up as bonus songs on a soundtrack album. Elvis also cut a very smooth re-make of Ketty Lester's 'Love Letters', earmarked for single release. A return to Nashville on June 12 saw Elvis add vocals to three music tracks done two days before. A sweeping ballad, 'Indescribably Blue', was a future A-side, as was a sentimental song written by Red West, 'If Every Day Was Like Christmas'. The third number was a ballad called 'I'll Remember You' from the pen of Hawaiian songwriter Kuiokalani Lee. Elvis was so pleased with these two sessions that he wrote a personal note to thank Felton and all the musicians.

It must have been dispiriting for Elvis to have to record the soundtrack for his next picture, *Double Trouble*. What enthusiasm could he muster for a weak song like 'Long Legged Girl' or the dreadful children's song 'Old MacDonald'? The film itself continued the general downward spiral. There was little to recommend the story of singer Guy Lambert's adventures in London and Belgium, involving a kidnapping and jewel thieves. Elvis, of course, didn't set foot in Europe. His leading lady was London teenager Annette Day, hand-picked by co-producer Judd Bernard. Another Brit on the cast was the late Norman Rossington, the only actor to have appeared in films with the trio of Elvis, The Beatles and Cliff Richard. As befitting a pro, Rossington gave a credible performance but when it was released audiences for *Double Trouble* were very sparse.

In September, 1966, Elvis leased a home in the desert retreat of Palm Springs. Colonel Parker already had a home there, along with the rich and famous, like Frank Sinatra, and Bob Hope.

Elvis made his final film for Hal Wallis that autumn, recording his poorest soundtrack yet on Paramount's recording stage. In *Easy Come Easy Go* Elvis played ex-navy frogman Ted Jackson searching for sunken treasure in murky waters. Cue long, boring underwater scenes with a stunt double. It was a sad end to his relationship with a studio that had served him so well earlier in his career.

In late 1966, Elvis began to take a keen interest in horses, buying several animals (one of which was a Christmas present for Priscilla), plus riding gear, refurbishing the large barn in his backyard, and riding around Graceland's grounds. He bought a diamond ring, too – and placed it on Priscilla's finger after he proposed to her just before Christmas. It was kept a secret from the press and fans, though. In fact, in the mid-Sixties, thanks largely

Elvis made his final film for Hal Wallis that autumn

to Col Parker's efficient screening mechanisms, it was very difficult to find out anything very much about Elvis's private life.

The horse-buying spree continued in 1967, and one special purchase was a palomino that Elvis named Rising Sun. His new interest needed more space than Graceland's grounds allowed, and before long he'd bought a 160-acre ranch just over the Mississippi border, some ten miles from Graceland, and named it the Circle G. Elvis and his buddies played at being cowboys. He purchased pickups for everyone and trailers for them to live in, while he lived in a small ranch house.

Reluctantly, Elvis tore himself away from the Circle G to do a session in Nashville on February 21, cutting songs for *Clambake*, his next movie for United Artists. The standout song in a rather dismal soundtrack was 'You Don't Know Me'. Elvis's departure for Hollywood was delayed because he was too intent on enjoying his new ranch. When he complained of saddle sores, he became acquainted with Dr George Nichopoulos, who would become his personal physician. At

length, Elvis flew out to California in early March, but there was a further delay when he had a fall in his bathroom at Rocca Place. Colonel Parker had had enough; he sent Larry Geller and his religious books packing, and read the riot act to the rest of the entourage.

Clambake was another poor film, even though Elvis had one of his favourite co-stars, Shelley Fabares, back for a third time. His role was of rich young man Scott Hayward who traded places with a water-ski instructor and won a speedboat race.

Below: The $6,000,000 Man Lee Majors seen here with Elvis in 1967 at Universal Studios. (Universal Pictures /Granlund)

From speedboat to *Speedway*. Our hero was stock-car race-driver Steve Grayson in his next effort, filmed for MGM in the summer. Nancy Sinatra played an Internal Revenue agent keeping tabs on his winnings, which his manager had been gambling away. The movie had another lack-lustre soundtrack.

Between the two movies, a very special event made headlines: Elvis and Priscilla were married at the Aladdin Hotel in Las Vegas on May 1. They'd flown in from Palm Springs in the early hours, obtained a marriage licence, and exchanged their vows in a ceremony attended by Vernon Presley, Priscilla's parents, and several of Elvis's friends. Joe Esposito and Marty Lacker acted as best men. Elvis wore a paisley patterned suit and his bride wore a white chiffon gown with seed pearl trim, and a tiara. Colonel Parker masterminded the wedding, causing resentment among some of the entourage, including Red West, who hadn't

been invited. The newlyweds seemed very happy, though, as they cut the large, tiered cake and toasted each other. A second reception was held at Graceland on May 29 for family and friends who weren't in Las Vegas, and Elvis and Priscilla donned their wedding attire again. Just a few weeks later, on the set of *Speedway*, a delighted Elvis announced that his new bride was pregnant. Presley fans welcomed the news, just as they had when they heard he'd got wed.

By August, Elvis had lost almost all interest in his ranch, and before too long, the horses were moved back to Graceland, the trailers and pickups disposed of, and the ranch eventually sold. Several of the Memphis Mafia were no longer with Elvis; Priscilla understandably wasn't too keen on having so many of the entourage around all the time.

Left: Priscilla and Elvis celebrate with a Wedding Breakfast at the Aladdin Hotel, Las Vegas May 1, 1967 (EPFC) Below: Nancy Sinatra, Nelson Rockerfeller, with Vernon & Dee Presley and Dee's three sons from a previous marriage on the set of Speedway (Tunzi)

As far as Elvis's recording career was concerned, there was light at the end of the tunnel. In September, 1967, at a session at Studio B, Elvis cut some tracks that pointed to a new enthusiasm and direction. 'Big Boss Man' and 'Hi-Heel Sneakers' were feisty numbers, and 'Guitar Man' benefited from having its composer, Jerry Reed, on the session, contributing his distinctive guitar style. Despite its more modern sound, 'Big Boss Man' only just scraped into

Between the two movies, a very special event made headlines

the Top 40. Recent record sales had been very disappointing. Only 'Love Letters', which reached No 19 in 1966, had sold reasonably well. Even *How Great Thou Art* had only reached No 18 earlier in 1967, although it became a long-term seller.

There was yet another film to be made, but at least MGM's *Stay Away, Joe* was unlike the formula movies of the past two years. It was a knockabout comedy adapted from the novel of the same name by Dan Cushman, and cast Elvis as modern day native American rodeo champion Joe Lightcloud, trying to help his family raise a herd of cattle.

He seemed to enjoy the role; much of the film seemed like one long party. The handful of songs didn't detract from the story. There were some genuinely funny scenes, such as when Joe's sister's future mother-in-law visits the ramshackle Lightcloud house. Elvis got good support from Burgess Meredith, Katy Jurado, and Joan Blondell, and there was authentic location footage shot in Arizona.

1968 dawned with much promise. Not only was Elvis about to become a father, but his manager had set up a deal with NBC for him to do his first TV special. Before the baby was born, Elvis spent a couple of days in Nashville, cutting Chuck Berry's lyrically clever 'Too Much Monkey Business' and

Above: On the set of Stay Away Joe *Elvis Presley proudly holds a greeting from British fans following a charity convention at the Palais, Nottingham, England on August 13, 1967 (EPFC)*

Above: Elvis renews his acquaintance with Line Renaud in December 1968 whom he had first met in Paris in January 1960 at the Lido show at the Casino de Paris. To the right is veteran actor Edward G. Robinson (Granlund / Jean-Marie Pouzenc)

another great Jerry Reed song, 'US Male', a song with attitude – some say an early attempt at white-rap. Reed again played guitar on the session. After its release in February, 'US Male' took Elvis back into the Top 30 for the first time in nearly two years.

On February 1, Priscilla gave birth to a healthy baby girl at Memphis Baptist Hospital. Elvis was overjoyed, and so were his fans, who thronged around the hospital entrance and the Graceland gates four days later, when Elvis took his wife and little daughter home. The couple had chosen the name Lisa Marie, and before long congratulatory cards and baby gifts began to arrive from all over the world.

Having rented a succession of homes in California, in February Elvis purchased his first home there, at 1174 Hillcrest Drive, on the Trousdale Estates, where only two of the entourage would live there with him. As they had done at previous homes, fans gathered at the gate in hopes of seeing Elvis, Priscilla, or Lisa Marie.

Elvis's role in his next film was, like that in *Stay Away Joe*, of a more adult nature. MGM had adapted Dan Greenburg's first novel, *Kiss My Firm But Pliant Lips*, for the screen as *Live A Little, Love A Little*. It told the story of the romance between a photographer and a kooky young woman. Elvis played Greg Nolan to Michelle Carey's Bernice/Alice… or whatever she felt like calling herself. With sleek sideburns, Elvis looked more like the Elvis of old, only more handsome, a man of the world. The handful of songs included 'Edge Of Reality' sung in a dream

sequence, a pop video years before they were invented. Vernon Presley had a cameo, non-speaking role in the film, which was partly shot on location in and around LA.

Back in September, 1965, Elvis had welcomed Tom Jones onto the set of *Paradise, Hawaiian Style*, and the two had struck up a friendship. Jones was playing Las Vegas in April, 1968, and Elvis took Priscilla and several friends to see his show at the Flamingo. The same month, Elvis spent Easter at his new rented home on Camino del Rey in Palm Springs. He didn't forget his first wedding anniversary; he sent flowers to Priscilla and organised a party at the Hillcrest house.

Prior to taping the TV special, Elvis took Priscilla and Lisa Marie to Hawaii, along with several friends. They stayed at the Ilikai on Waikiki Beach, and attended a karate tournament staged by Ed Parker, whom Elvis had first met in the early Sixties.

Much of June was spent in rehearsal for the TV special, which would be titled *Elvis*. Bob Finkel was the producer and he hired creative young director Steve Binder, while Bones Howe was musical director. The Colonel's initial idea for a Christmas special was abandoned after Binder

1968 dawned with much promise

proposed that the key element of the show should be a jam session before an invited audience, with Elvis's old sidemen, Scotty Moore and DJ Fontana, in the band. Elvis laughed and joked and sang many of his old hits and a few new songs in two informal shows taped at NBC Studios in Burbank, California on June 27. 'Tiger Man' was a highlight of the second show. For these sequences, Elvis wore a black leather two-piece designed by Bill Belew. Two days later, two more shows were done in front of the invited audience (including Priscilla) and Elvis wore the sexy black leather outfit again, but this time was alone on the small, square stage. At all shows, he looked very happy to be back in front of an audience, singing his heart out. Production sequences were filmed on June 28 and 30, together with a gospel segment and a storyline built around 'Guitar Man'. A

bordello scene was edited out before the special was aired. To conclude the show, Elvis performed an impassioned new song, 'If I Can Dream'.

Above: On April 6, 1968 Elvis and Priscilla meet Tom Jones at the Flamingo Hotel, Las Vegas after his sell out show in the casino showroom. (Tom Jones) Right: During the filming of The Trouble With Girls *from MGM, Elvis accepts an award from the British Guide Dogs For The Blind Association on behalf of fund raising achievements by the British Fan Club. This picture is autographed by Elvis. (Todd Slaughter)*

Once the taping was completed – and Elvis had every reason to be pleased at the outcome – there were only a few weeks before he had to start work on his next film. *Charro!* was made for National General, and in July Elvis went on location to Arizona. He'd grown a beard for his role as reformed outlaw Jess Wade, framed for the theft of a valuable Mexican cannon. Ina Balin and Victor French gave good support, but the film wasn't as exciting as it promised to be. The only music was the dramatic title song, sung over the credits.

Elvis liked this role and so too did those fans who were able to view it despite its limited distribution.

While Elvis was relaxing in Memphis before starting yet another movie, Dewey Phillips died on September 28, aged 42, and three days later Elvis attended his funeral.

The final film of the year (and, in fact, Elvis's final MGM movie), was *The Trouble With Girls (And How To Get Into It)*, based on a book called *Chautauqua* by Day Keene and Dwight Vincent. Dressed Twenties style in a white suit and fedora, Elvis looked dashing as Walter Hale, manager of a travelling Chautauqua company. His co-stars were Marlyn Mason and Sheree North. The film's few songs included the gospel number, 'Swing Down, Sweet Chariot'. The trouble with *The Trouble With Girls* was… not enough Elvis in many scenes.

The ratings for the Singer-sponsored TV special when

it aired on December 3 were massive. In just 60 minutes, Elvis's career was regenerated and his fans were ecstatic. The soundtrack album climbed up to No 8, while 'If I Can Dream' got to No 12. The show became known as the '68

At all shows, he looked very happy to be back in front of an audience

Comeback Special and was a watershed in Elvis's career.

Elvis certainly had plenty to celebrate at Christmas and at his annual New Year's Eve party in Memphis, and things just got better from now on. In January and February, 1969, Elvis undertook recording sessions at American

Studios in Memphis, using their talented "house" musicians and cutting over thirty songs in all, tracks that are undoubtedly among the best work of his career. In a voice that echoed the hunger of his early years yet resonated with a new maturity, Elvis was truly inspired on songs like 'Long Black Limousine', 'I'll Hold You In My Heart', 'Stranger In My Own Home Town', 'Only The Strong Survive', 'Any Day Now', 'After Loving You' and others. There was a need for him to consolidate his return to the charts after 'If I Can Dream', and the tracks which did the trick were 'In The Ghetto' (his first US Top 10 entry in four years at No 3, and a UK No 1), 'Kentucky Rain', 'Don't Cry Daddy', and best of all, the compelling 'Suspicious Minds', which restored him to No 1

Above: A bearded Elvis Presley on the set of Charro *with producer/director Charles Marquis Warren (Warren/National General Pictures)*

in the USA. The album, *From Elvis In Memphis*, although it only got to No 16, is considered to be Elvis's greatest album by many fans and critics alike.

In between the two sessions, Elvis took a break with his family in snowy Aspen, Colorado, and celebrated Lisa Marie's first birthday. Once the sessions were completed, it was back to Hollywood. There was just one more film to do before Elvis was free to do what he had been hankering to do – perform live shows again. The film, for Universal, was prophetically titled *Change Of Habit*, and at least Elvis's movie career ended on a high note. It was a drama in which – looking handsomer than ever – he played Dr John Carpenter, working in a deprived area and encountering serious social issues. His co-star was TV's popular Mary Tyler Moore, playing one of three nuns working undercover as nurses. The film had tension and a few lighter moments, just four songs, and a memorable, moving rage reduction scene between Elvis and an autistic child. *Change Of Habit* came too late, though; by this time, Presley films were being screened as B-movies, if they were being screened at all, in the UK, at least. In fact, *Change Of Habit* had its British premiere on BBC 1 in August, 1971,

Above: Baseball ace Duke Snyder visits Elvis on the set of The Trouble With Girls *in 1968 (MGM)*
Below: Gospel singer Mahalia Jackson visits the set of Change Of Habit *and meets both Elvis and his co-star Barbara McNair (Universal Pictures)*

though it enjoyed a public premiere when it was screened by the British Fan Club at the Theatre Nouveau, in the Grande Duchy of Luxembourg, at a European Fan Club Convention which was filmed in part by MGM.

ELVIS

CHAPTER 10
"VIVA LAS VEGAS"

In Las Vegas in 1969, a huge new hotel called the International was being built, and the news that Elvis was going to perform there caused great excitement among Presley fans. Elvis was filmed in front of the half-built hotel in late February, supposedly signing his contract (the actual contract was signed in April). Much preparation needed to be done, not least getting a band together.

GATHERING THE LEGENDS

Before the serious business of choosing the musicians, though, Elvis had time to relax in the summer. He divided his time between Hawaii (including a stay at Coco Palms on Kauai), LA, Palm Springs, Las Vegas and Memphis. At home, he rode around his Graceland estate and met the many fans who gathered daily at the Music Gates.

Since Scotty, DJ, and The Jordanaires didn't fancy leaving Nashville, legendary Shreveport guitarist James Burton was chosen to lead a band that comprised pianist Larry Muhoberac, bass player Jerry Scheff, rhythm guitarist John Wilkinson and Dallas drummer Ronnie Tutt. Charlie Hodge was added to the line-up, ostensibly to play guitar and harmonise with Elvis, but also as an on-stage assistant to hand him glasses of water or Gatorade, take care of gifts handed up to

Left: Radio Luxembourg DJ Peter Aldersley accepts a tandem bike featured in the movie Elvis: That's The Way It Is. *(EPFC)*
Below: Elvis signs for his first live appearances at the International Hotel in Las Vegas (later to become the Las Vegas Hilton) in 1969. Hotel president Alex Shoofey is to the left with Bill Miller on Elvis' right (International Hotel)

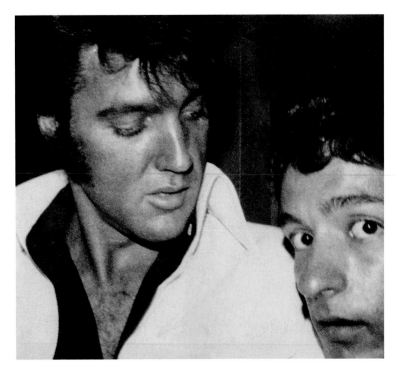

There could be no doubt who was making a comeback and who was in town! Elvis was very nervous, but once the opening acts – The Sweet Inspirations and comedian Sammy Shore – left the stage, Elvis received a tumultuous welcome from the packed, 2000-strong celebrity-laden audience. All nerves disappeared once he'd sung his first couple of songs and he put on a show that thrilled everyone.

'Blue Suede Shoes' got the show off to a rocking, rolling start, and Elvis continued with 'I Got A Woman', then the big hits came one after the other: 'Love Me Tender', 'Jailhouse Rock', 'Don't Be Cruel', 'Heartbreak Hotel', 'All Shook Up' and 'Hound Dog'. He calmed things down with 'Memories', first heard on the TV special, and got people tapping their toes to 'My Babe'. 'I Can't Stop Loving You' and 'In The Ghetto' showcased his contrasting styles. Elvis could sing anything and make it his own. 'Suspicious Minds' was nothing short of a revelation, as Elvis extended the song, giving it a real workout. (It hadn't yet been released on disc.) There was more: a Beatles medley of

Elvis (and, later on, to hand him endless scarves to pass out to clamouring fans). Charlie was also useful in helping Elvis choose the play list. To round out the sound, Elvis picked

Above: French fan club president Jean-Marc Garguillo meets Elvis backstage in Las Vegas 1969 (Garguillo)
Right: One hit wonder ('Big Bad John') Jimmy Dean seen with Elvis in 1971. Elvis is seen wearing his Vegas Gold Championship belt and his Jaycees mediallion. (Granlund)

The Imperials and an all black female soul group The Sweet Inspirations, plus Millie Kirkham, a soprano used on many of his recording sessions. The International's orchestra under the direction of Bobby Morris would complete the on-stage line-up. Elvis asked Bill Belew to design his stage wear, and Belew, of the IC Costume Company in Hollywood, came up with black or white two-piece outfits based on karate gis.

Rehearsals began at RCA's Sunset Boulevard studio in mid-July, moving to the International a few days later. Once Barbra Streisand, who'd opened the hotel, had finished her engagement, and ironed out all the tweaks and peaks in the newly installed sound system, rehearsals

The audience had witnessed an historic show

continued in the showroom – the biggest in town – with final dress rehearsals on opening night, July 31.

Those arriving in Las Vegas for the invitation-only opening show were met by posters and banners and all sorts of promotional advertising ideas thought up by Tom Parker.

'Yesterday' and 'Hey Jude', Chuck Berry's 'Johnny B Goode', and back to his roots for 'Mystery Train' and then 'Tiger Man'. A wild 'What'd I Say' brought the crowd to its feet, and Elvis disappeared behind the gold curtain, only to reappear and sing one final song, 'Can't Help Falling In Love'.

Below Elvis with his Jaycees Award and medallion after the ceremony in Memphis on January 16, 1971. On his left is Boston City Council Leader Thomas Atkins - another of the "Ten Outstanding Young Men of the Year" recipients (Memphis Bureau of Tourism)

The audience had witnessed an historic show (which RCA seems not to have had the foresight to record), and an elated Elvis returned backstage after a standing ovation. The press were already looking for superlatives to describe the event. At a press conference held afterwards, Elvis said it had been one of the most exciting nights of his life. He had wanted to return to live concerts because "I missed the live contact with an audience. It was getting harder and harder to sing to a camera all day."

For the next four weeks, Elvis did two shows nightly (dinner and cocktail shows), and between August 21-26 RCA made live recordings under Felton Jarvis's supervision. By this time, a more relaxed Elvis was including a long, often humorous monologue about his career, and singing a wider selection of songs. RCA taped 'Words', 'Are You Lonesome Tonight' (including a laughing version), and other songs, plus all the well-known hits. Many of the live tracks formed the Vegas part of *From Memphis To Vegas/From Vegas To Memphis*, Elvis's first double album, issued in October, 1969. (The Memphis part comprised recently recorded songs not included on *From Elvis In Memphis*.)

By the time Elvis closed his record-breaking appearance on August 28, he'd played to 101,500 people and grossed over $1,500,000, another Vegas record. The hotel presented Elvis with a gold, diamond studded championship belt.

With time on his hands, Elvis spent the rest of the year

commuting between his favourite places – LA, Vegas, Palm Springs, and Memphis, and in October took Priscilla and several friends to Hawaii on a trip financed by the International, as their way of saying "thank you". Elvis's plans to continue his vacation in Europe were scuppered by Colonel Parker, who thought that fans wouldn't like it if Elvis didn't perform. Instead, Elvis holidayed in Nassau, in the laid-back Bahamas.

A second season in Las Vegas was set up for early 1970, when the first jumpsuits made their appearance. They were black or white, with macramé belts and different trims, and were again designed by Bill Belew. The engagement began on January 26, and Larry Muhoberac was replaced by Glen

on closing night, Elvis was on stage for well over his allotted time

D. Hardin on piano, while Ronnie Tutt left (temporarily) and Bob Lanning took over as drummer.

Elvis's repertoire now included 'Sweet Caroline', 'The Wonder Of You', 'Let It Be Me', 'Proud Mary' and new showstopper 'Polk Salad Annie'. RCA made recordings in mid-February for an album called *On Stage*, which was released in June. On closing night, February 23, Elvis was

on stage for well over his allotted time (55 minutes to an hour), and gave what was later called a "fans'" show, singing 'Lawdy Miss Clawdy' and 'Blueberry Hill' at the piano.

As a first step towards going out on tour, Elvis played six shows at the huge Astrodome in Houston on February 27 and 28, and March 1 as part of the Houston Livestock Show and Rodeo. The conditions weren't ideal; he had to perform on a stage in the middle of the vast arena and the sound was poor. But the record-breaking crowds were just happy to see him. The Saturday evening performance drew an amazing 43,614 people. While he was in Houston, Elvis gave a couple of press conferences and was presented with several gold awards for recent hits.

After renting out homes in Palm Springs, in early April Elvis bought a house at 845 Chino Canyon Road, and a few days later, treated himself to a new car, a black Mercedes limousine.

Above: Elvis, again wearing his Gold Championship belt and his Jaycees medallion, poses with Joe Moscheo, Terry Blackwood, Jim Murray, and Armond Morales (Imperials Quartet) with songwriter Larry Gatlin (Tunzi) Right: Elvis and country music giant Glen Campbell admire Elvis' torch in his suite at the International Hotel in 1971 (Granlund)

A mammoth recording session took place at Studio B between June 4-8. Producer Felton Jarvis was now working full time for Elvis, and James Burton played on the session. Amongst almost three dozen songs cut, there were several selections for a country-themed album, songs for new singles, and tunes for an album to be released in conjunction with a unique movie project. Songs chosen for

Luxembourg to film at the European fan clubs' convention on September 5, hosted by the British club and supported by Tony Prince and Radio Luxembourg. A good many of Elvis's British fans were present, and were in great spirits because 'The Wonder Of You' was topping the UK charts.

Left: Mona Granlund, wife of Norwegian Fan Club president Pal Granlund presents Elvis with a platinum album award from RCA Oslo (Granlund)
Right: In 1971 Elvis became a proud owner of the first Italian hand-made Stutz Blackhawk car imported into the United States. (Tunzi)

For this season at the International, Joe Guercio took over as orchestra leader, and Ronnie Tutt was back behind the drums. Partway through the season, after the MGM crew and cameras had left, Kathy Westmoreland ("The little girl with the beautiful high voice" as Elvis often called her) took over from Millie Kirkham, who returned permanently to Nashville. New songs this time around included 'Bridge Over Troubled Water', a medley of 'Little Sister'/'Get Back', 'You've Lost That Lovin' Feelin'', 'Just Pretend' and the beautiful 'I Just Can't Help Believin''. Several new white jumpsuits made their debut, and a fringed outfit was especially admired by fans. After the final show on September 7, Elvis went out on the road, appearing in six cities, starting off in Phoenix on the 9th, and taking in St Louis, Detroit, Miami Beach, and Tampa, and winding up in Mobile. Audiences everywhere welcomed him warmly, and he revelled in being back amongst his grass roots fans. For his Seventies tours, Elvis had no choice but to fly from city to city.

Elvis Country included 'Faded Love', a wonderfully laid-back 'Funny How Time Slips Away' and 'Little Cabin On The Hill'. Tracks destined for singles included 'I've Lost You' and 'You Don't Have To Say You Love Me'. In fact, Elvis cut enough songs to fill a further album to be titled *Love Letters*, with his "leftovers".

THAT'S THE WAY IT IS

It had been decided that MGM would document Elvis Presley in concert, capturing Elvis both in rehearsal and on stage at the International. Called *Elvis: That's The Way It Is*, it would enable fans all over the world to see his scintillating Vegas show. Rehearsals at MGM's Culver City studios in July were filmed. More rehearsals (not filmed) took place at RCA's Sunset Boulevard studio. The final rehearsals at the International were also filmed. A nervous Elvis was seen before the opening show on August 10, and that show and several subsequent shows were filmed in part by director Denis Sanders. Some of Elvis's Californian fans were filmed for "cut-ins" in the movie, as well as staff at the International. Sanders even sent a film crew over to

Audiences everywhere welcomed him warmly

Before the next tour got underway, Elvis did a short recording session in Nashville on September 22, cutting just four songs, including 'Whole Lotta Shakin' Goin' On' and 'Snowbird', to complete his forthcoming country album. He was made a deputy sheriff of Shelby County, Tennessee (licensed to carry a firearm), and bought himself an expensive black Italian Stutz car. He also put down a deposit on a new Californian home at 144 Monovale Drive in Holmby Hills, and began to give gold TCB/lightning bolt pendants to members of his entourage, musicians, and others, for helping him take care of business… in a flash. Ladies close to Elvis later got TLC (Tender Loving Care) necklaces.

The next tour began on November 10 in Oakland, and took in several cities on the West Coast before finishing in Denver. One notable show was at the Inglewood Forum in

Above: RCA's George Parkhill presents Elvis with an award for 3 million sales of the album Live At Madison Square Garden - *Elvis's only live album recorded in New York City at the time. (RCA)*

LA, where Elvis wore a spectacular outfit with batwing sleeves with very long fringes, and he rather uncharacteristically reminded the crowd that he had 56 gold singles and 14 gold albums, and had sold 200 million records.

While Elvis was out on tour, *That's The Way It Is* opened in the USA on November 11. (Fans in Europe wouldn't be able to see it until the following spring). The film was a revelation. The Elvis of *That's The Way It Is* was quite unlike the Elvis of the Sixties movies. The way he looked, the way he sang, the way he moved – everything about him was different. He looked, as he had done on the Comeback Special, the king of cool. The only annoying thing about the film was the cut-ins of fans. (In 2000, a Special Edition of the film was released minus the irritating cut-ins, and included extra rehearsal and on stage footage. Prior to this, in 1992, a video called *The Lost Performances* included many songs not included in the original film, as well as fascinating rehearsal scenes.)

Goaded by his father and Priscilla about overspending, on December 19, Elvis flew (on his own) from Memphis to Washington, DC, from there to LA to pick up his friend Jerry Schilling, and back next day to Washington, where another friend, Sonny West, joined them. An extraordinary turn of events took place. Elvis left a letter for President Nixon at the White House in the early morning of December 21. A meeting was granted, and later that day Elvis was shown into the Oval Office and proceeded to show Nixon recent photos of Priscilla and Lisa Marie. He asked Nixon to help get a coveted Federal Narcotics Officers' badge (he was an avid collector of law enforcement badges), and introduced his two friends to the President. After a Christmas spent at Graceland, Elvis returned to Washington on December 30 with several friends and next day was given a special tour of FBI HQ, then flew home to attend his annual New Year's Eve party.

Every year, the Jaycees (Junior Chambers of Commerce) chose their outstanding ten young men in the nation. Elvis was nominated and picked as one of 1970's honourees. Ceremonies took place in Memphis on January 16, 1971. A prayer breakfast at the Holiday Inn-Rivermont, on the banks of the Mississippi, was followed by a reception for the award winners at Graceland, a dinner hosted by Elvis at a Memphis restaurant, and an awards ceremony at the Ellis Auditorium in the evening. Elvis graciously accepted his award – a silver-coloured pair of hands and a matching medallion – and told the assembly that "Every dream I've ever dreamed has come true a hundred times", and he quoted from the well-known song, 'Without A Song'.

Season four in Las Vegas kicked off on January 26, and for the first time, '2001, A Space Odyssey' was used prior to Elvis's entrance on stage. A highlight of the shows was 'How Great Thou Art', and the Vegas audiences responded enthusiastically to this powerfully sung gospel song. Elvis sang 'The Impossible Dream' as his closing song this time around.

At a short session at Studio B in March, Elvis recorded 'Amazing Grace' and three other songs before the session was called off after Elvis was admitted to hospital and diagnosed with glaucoma. Two months later, he returned to Nashville and undertook a six-day session primarily to cut Christmas and gospel songs, followed by a third session in June to cut more gospel tracks. In October, 1971, the seasonal tracks were released on *Elvis Sings The Wonderful World Of Christmas*, an album notable for its childlike sleeve design, but also for the great blues, 'Merry Christmas Baby'. Most Presley singles and albums were no longer getting high chart placings. Even the beautiful 'I'm Leavin", June's single release, only reached No 36. The Christmas album never even charted.

Elvis's birthplace in Tupelo had been renovated and furniture from the Thirties gave it an authentic look inside. On June 1, it opened to the public. Not to be outdone, the Memphis City Council announced that a 12-mile stretch of

Elvis had a new address: 3764 Elvis Presley Boulevard

Highway 51 South would henceforth be known as Elvis Presley Boulevard. When it was officially dedicated in early 1972, Elvis had a new address: 3764 Elvis Presley Boulevard.

The only other nightclub that Elvis played in the Seventies was the Sahara in Lake Tahoe, in picturesque northern Nevada, overlooking the lakeside and facing the Golden State of California across the water. His first season there, in the High Sierra Room, was for two weeks, starting on July 20. The smaller showroom was packed nightly. By

closing night, August 2, Elvis had broken attendance records. Just seven days later, he opened at the newly renamed Las Vegas Hilton. His costumes were getting flashier, with gold studs and glitter. At the closing show on September 6, he wore a cape for the first time. Towards the end of the season, on

Above: President Richard Nixon meets the King in the Oval office at the White House, Washington DC on December 21, 1970. (The Nixon Archives)

August 28, Elvis became the proud recipient of a Lifetime Achievement Award from the National Academy of Recording Arts and Sciences.

He went on tour in November, thrilling sell-out crowds in a dozen cities, including Cleveland, Boston, and Dallas, and wearing studded and glittery jumpsuits of black or white with matching capes. The Imperials were replaced by JD Sumner and The Stamps. As a teenager, Elvis had met deep-voiced Sumner at gospel singin's in Memphis in the 1950s.

For all the success of concerts at hotels in Nevada and elsewhere on the road, things were starting to go wrong in Elvis's personal life. Relations between Elvis and Priscilla were strained over Christmas, and she flew out to LA with Lisa Marie leaving Elvis to host a small New Year's Eve party at Graceland.

During Elvis's next season at the Hilton, from January 26 to February 23, 1972, RCA made live recordings. New

to Elvis's act was 'It's Over', and 'You Gave Me A Mountain', which he always insisted had nothing to do with his marriage break up. There was another new showstopper, the patriotic 'An American Trilogy' which segued three anthemic melodies in 'Dixie', 'Battle Hymn Of The Republic' and 'All My Trials'.

A second documentary was filmed by MGM in the spring, following Elvis and company as they played vast arenas across the USA. *Elvis On Tour* also showed Elvis in rehearsal in the RCA studio in LA, backstage at some venues, and Vernon Presley was filmed at Graceland. Some Fifties footage supplied by the British fan club rounded out a fascinating film. A split screen technique was used, and Elvis gave producers Pierre Adidge and Robert Abel an interview, parts of which were used as voiceovers in the film. *Elvis On Tour* didn't do as well as *That's The Way It Is* at the box office. It was more of a "fans'" film – and the fans loved it! It was chosen as Best Documentary of 1972, winning a Golden Globe Award.

Left: Paul Anka (right) with his manager (centre) and Elvis in Las Vegas August 1972 (Granlund) Right: Actor comedian and singer Jimmy Durante backstage with Elvis in Las Vegas 1972 (Granlund)

Just before the start of the filming, Elvis had recorded at RCA's Hollywood studio, using most of his on stage musicians on a recording session for the first time. Among the songs cut were two future classics, 'Always On My Mind' and 'Burning Love', plus a song that Red West had co-written called 'Separate Ways', which could only allude to Elvis's separation from Priscilla.

While Elvis was being filmed on tour in April, 'He Touched Me' was released. The quality of the gospel album was never in doubt, with beautiful songs like 'An Evening Prayer' and 'A Thing Called Love', and this perennial seller won Elvis his second Grammy.

The next tour got off to a flying start with four sold-out shows at New York's Madison Square Garden between June

criticism of his movements in the Fifties, he replied, "Man, I was tame compared to what they do now… I didn't do anything but just jiggle!"

RCA recorded both of the shows on June 10. The evening show was rush-released on LP on June 18, and got to No 11 in the charts, going gold. The rest of the June tour saw sell-out arena after sell-out arena.

By the end of July, the news had broken about Elvis's separation from Priscilla. Scaremongers put out rumours about him being so upset that he was going to cancel his up-coming engagement in Vegas. A large party of fans from the British Fan Club, about to go on their first trip to the USA and attend shows at the Hilton, were fervently hoping the rumours weren't true. They need not have worried. Elvis was a professional. The show(s) would go on. And anyway, he had a stunning new girlfriend, Memphis beauty queen Linda Thompson.

Elvis said that it was very hard to live up to an image

9 and 11. Some 80,000 people witnessed these historic concerts, and Elvis charmed the tough New York crowds – and the press. The *New York Times's* review ended, "… a champion, the only one in his class". Before the concerts, there was a press conference at the New York Hilton, when Elvis said that it was very hard to live up to an image, and very hard to find any good new material. Asked about the

CHAPTER 11
"THE DAYS GROW LONGER AND THE NIGHTS – WELL THE NIGHTS HAVE A THOUSAND EYES"

Elvis opened at the Hilton on August 4, 1972 varying his stage attire by wearing suits with coloured shirts. New songs included 'What Now My Love', 'My Way', 'I'll Remember You', and 'Fever'. After the trauma of his marriage break-up, he was encouraged by the support of his fans. By the time that the British Fan Club arrived in Las Vegas, after first visiting Nashville, Tupelo, and Memphis, Elvis was back to wearing caped jumpsuits. Fans were able to attend several shows, and once they'd figured out the tipping system, many secured seats by the stage. Fan Club boss Todd Slaughter, Radio Luxembourg's Tony Prince, and a few of the group met Elvis backstage.

Below: Ten passengers on the first British fan club trip meet the King on September 4, 1972. Altogether about a third of the passengers on that inaugural trip managed to talk Colonel Parker in allowing them back stage. (EPFC)

Elvis live was phenomenal. Records didn't do his expressive voice justice. Photographs didn't do him – or his glittering outfits – justice. Fortunate indeed were fans who saw Elvis perform live. Even better was to get a kiss, or a scarf from around his neck, which was enjoyed and cherished by Anne E. Nixon. The showroom's stage lighting added greatly to dramatic songs like 'You've Lost That Lovin' Feelin'', the sexy 'Fever' or the exciting 'Mystery Train'/'Tiger Man' sequence. Once you'd seen Elvis live, you wanted to see him again and again.

A UNIQUE CONCERT

After the closing show on September 4, Elvis gave a press conference in the Hilton's 30th floor ballroom to promote a unique concert he was performing the following January,

Right: Radio Luxembourg DJ Tony Prince and British Fan Club secretary Todd Slaughter present Elvis Presley with a New Musical Express Award for The World's Greatest Entertainer category in the pop paper's annual readers' poll. Prince recorded a rare interview for 208. (EPFC)

"Aloha From Hawaii Via Satellite". "It's hard to comprehend that happening, to all the countries all over the world," he said, adding that live concerts were his favourite part of the business.

'Burning Love' was released in August, and reached No 2, adding yet another gold disc to Elvis's collection.

Above: Italian Fan Club president Livio Monari backstage with Elvis in Las Vegas August 1972 (Monari)

Elvis's November tour included dates in Hawaii at the HIC (Honolulu International Centre), the same venue that would be used for the satellite telecast. The shows completed, at the Hawaiian Village Hotel on November 20, there was another press conference to announce that the satellite

show would be a benefit for the Kui Lee Cancer Fund. "It's a great privilege to do this satellite show," Elvis said, "and I'm gonna do my best, and all the people that work for me, to do a good show. It's just pure entertainment, no messages… just try and make people happy for that one hour that it comes across. If we do that, then I think we've done our job."

Elvis travelled to Hawaii on January 9, 1973, and began rehearsals. Producer/Director Marty Pasetta had designed a set at the HIC that included a ramp. As a safeguard, a full dress rehearsal with an audience was taped on Friday, January 12, but the live show in the early hours of Sunday, January 14 went without a hitch. At both shows, Elvis wore a striking white jumpsuit and cape with a patriotic eagle motif in red, blue, and gold stones, and accepted leis from fans who gathered round the ramp. Elvis gave the audience in the HIC and the 500 million viewers in the Far East and Australasia a programme that ranged from Fifties classics to new songs like 'Steamroller Blues' and 'Welcome To My World'. After announcing that the audience had donated $75,000 for the Kui Lee Cancer Fund, Elvis sang Lee's lovely 'I'll Remember You' to warm applause. After the audience had left, Elvis sang several more songs for inclusion in the Special when it was shown in the USA. Viewers there had to wait until April 4, when NBC screened a 90-minute show which got massive ratings. Several European countries screened the 60-minute show in the days following the telecast. A double LP of the *Aloha* show was released in February, which took Elvis back to No 1 in the US album charts for the first time since 1965.

Hot on the heels of his satellite triumph, Elvis returned

Right: Las Vegas February 17, 1973: Following the "Aloha From Hawaii" telecast, Honolulu International Centre Manager Matt Esposito presents Elvis with an award from the American Cancer Society for raising $75,000 for the Kui Lee Cancer Fund.

"It's a great privilege to do this satellite show"

to the Hilton, and between January 26 and February 23 delighted the fans who packed the showroom nightly, although a bout of illness forced cancellation of a few

Above: Christina and Börje Lundburg - a Swedish newspaper reporter with Elvis backstage at the Hilton in September 1973 (Expressen)

shows. At one show, four men got on stage and were repelled by an enraged Elvis and his bodyguards. A ramp had been added in the showroom, which would remain for Elvis's next few seasons there.

When Elvis began his next tour in April, bassist Emory Gordy replaced Jerry Scheff. Elvis did a second season at the Sahara Tahoe in May, which included a special 3 am Mother's Day show to benefit a local hospital. Illness forced him to cancel the last few days of the engagement.

Because fans were in danger of pulling him offstage, during his cross-country tour in July, Elvis stopped wearing capes. Later that month, Lisa Marie arrived at Graceland to spend the holidays with her father.

On July 20, Elvis went into Stax Studios in Memphis (American had closed by this time). James Burton and Ronnie Tutt helped lift what is generally regarded as a disappointing session, although Elvis cut funky songs like 'If You Don't Come Back' and 'Find Out What's Happening'. He returned to Stax in December, 1973, and cut some superior tracks that included 'Loving Arms', 'Good Time

Charlie's Got The Blues', and Chuck Berry's 'Promised Land'.

The members of the British Fan Club who saw Elvis perform at the Hilton that summer were treated to some fine shows. Elvis was in good spirits, joking and ad-libbing words to songs. Todd Slaughter and Luxembourg DJ Tony Prince met him backstage again. The only drawback for fans who saw several shows was having to listen to the same jokes from comedian Jackie Kahane, who'd been with Elvis since 1971. The engagement ran from August 6 to

Elvis was in good spirits, joking and ad-libbing words to songs

September 3, and was Elvis's last 4-week season.

There were newspaper headlines when Elvis and Priscilla were divorced at Santa Monica Courthouse on October 9. Pictures showed them walking out of the building arm in arm. More headlines a few days later said that Elvis was in Baptist Memorial Hospital in Memphis for tests. The hospital stay lasted for two weeks. By Christmas, he seemed to be in good health again.

SELLING THE LEGACY

In 1973, Colonel Parker controversially sold the rights to Elvis's pre-1973 recordings to RCA for $5.4 million, thus denying Elvis future royalties from his classic back catalogue. It seemed that Elvis and the Colonel had sold the family jewels as a short term answer to the spiralling debts accrued by both parties. Elvis' lavish spending on gifts for those in his circle, and the poor and needy, and Colonel Tom's addiction to

Above: Muhammad Ali spurs with Elvis in his Hilton Hotel suite in Las Vegas in February 1973. Elvis gives Ali an embroidered robe, and Ali gives Elvis a pair of signed boxing gloves. (Granlund)

'Spanish Eyes' and 'Let Me Be There', a new bass player, Duke Bardwell, and an additional vocal group, Voice. Following the closing show on February 9, Elvis set out on tour, and played the Houston Astrodome again, beating his own 1970 record, when 44,175 people witnessed the Saturday evening show on March 3.

Right: Jackie Wilson best known for his single 'Reet Petite' with Elvis in 1974 (Granlund)

Several shows took place in Memphis's Mid South Coliseum, and RCA recorded the final one on March 20. *Elvis As Recorded Live On Stage In Memphis* was released in July and showed Elvis in good voice and spirits entertaining his hometown fans. More importantly, the live version of 'How Great Thou Art' on the album won Elvis his third Grammy for "Best Inspirational Performance". A short tour of California in May was followed by eleven days at Lake Tahoe, although Elvis missed some shows due to illness.

Elvis had a No 17 hit in the summer with 'If You Talk In Your Sleep', co-written by Red West and recorded at Stax the previous December.

A 25-show tour across the USA in June saw Elvis playing to sell-out crowds. Linda Thompson, meanwhile, began redecorating Graceland, adding red carpet, curtains, and chairs, plus furry rugs and mirrors. Elvis had stained glass peacocks incorporated into the doors to the Music Room and on a whim, re-furnished his den with Hawaiian-styled carved furniture and artefacts.

When he opened in Las Vegas on January 26, he looked fine

gambling and gaming machines, had left them both without funds and little equity. When Elvis's portion of this sale was further reduced by Col Tom's commission and taxes, it seemed a poor price for his life's work – one of the most valuable catalogues in the history of popular music.

Above: September 2, 1973. Todd Slaughter presents Elvis with a further NME award for Top Male Vocalist before the Dinner Show at the Las Vegas Hilton (EPFC)
Right: Swedish music journalist Sten Berglind with Elvis at the Hilton 1973 (Expressen)

For the next few years, Elvis did little else but tour the USA. Despite hopes of a world tour, it never happened. Rumours abounded that Colonel Parker was an illegal Dutch immigrant without a US passport and that he was afraid to allow Elvis to tour abroad for rear of losing control of "his boy". Only a minority of fans could afford to travel to America to see Elvis. His reluctance to set foot in a recording studio meant that RCA had to rely heavily on live recordings. The Colonel turned down movie offers, notably *A Star Is Born* with Barbra Streisand in 1975.

In 1974, rumours were rife that Elvis was seriously overweight. When he opened in Las Vegas on January 26, he looked fine, and had new crowd-pleasing songs like

Above: Colonel Parker links arms with Mrs Wallace and Governor George backstage with Elvis in Alabama March 6, 1974. Granlund)

It soon became known as the Jungle Room.

The annual Summer Festival in Vegas ran from August 19-September 2, and was memorable for Elvis talking about many subjects including drugs rumours, and doing karate demos built around 'If You Talk In Your Sleep', plus long lectures on the martial art at some shows. He missed a couple of shows due to illness. British Fan Club members, on a third trip to Vegas, had been concerned about stories in the press but were relieved to find Elvis in good form with a just a slight paunch. He was doing a pounding 'Big Boss Man' and a new ballad about lost love called 'It's Midnight'. When Priscilla and Lisa Marie attended the closing show (along with Elvis's new girlfriend Sheila Ryan, who temporarily replaced Linda), during 'It's Midnight' Elvis urged, "Listen, Cilla". He wore sexy two-piece soft leather outfits before reverting back to jumpsuits for the last few shows. Several

Above: Elvis with J.D. Sumner (to his right) and members of the Stamps Quartet (Universal Management)

elaborately embroidered jumpsuits with eagle, tiger, or dragon motif were inspired by Elvis's interest in karate. In fact, he wanted to make a documentary about karate. He had risen to 8th degree black belt by August, 1974, his main instructors being Ed Parker in California and Master Kang Rhee in Memphis. Some filming was done in Memphis in

It was **evident** that **something** was **wrong**

September, but Elvis eventually lost interest and the project was never completed.

'Promised Land' gave Elvis a No 14 hit in the autumn, and he was off again on another tour from September 27 to October 9, but some of the shows left fans disappointed and

it was evident that something was wrong. He played shows at Lake Tahoe in mid-October to make up for those missed through illness in May.

On January 8, 1975, Elvis turned 40, spending his birthday quietly at Graceland. His return to Vegas was delayed due to poor health, and on January 29, he was admitted to Baptist Hospital with "breathing difficulties". Just days later, his father (who'd separated from his wife in 1974) had a heart attack and was admitted to the same hospital. It was February 14 before Elvis was allowed home. He had the satisfaction of seeing 'My Boy' – another Stax song – reach No 20.

Elvis finally returned to the recording studios between March 10 and 12, cutting tracks for a new album, *Today*, at RCA's Hollywood studio. He was in fine form, recording

tracks that varied from the catchy 'I Can Help' to the introspective 'Pieces Of My Life'.

Above: Elvis with his Memphis karate instructor Master Kang Rhee in 1974 at Rhee's Memphis dojo. Elvis funded filming for a "New Gladiators" documentary project but the movie was never completed. (EPFC)

He was back at the Hilton between March 18 and April 1, then spent most of the summer touring. A show in Jackson, Mississippi, on May 5 raised over $100,000 for victims of a tornado that had devastated McComb, Mississippi, in January. Bassist Jerry Scheff rejoined the band. Elvis was carrying some extra weight, which was accentuated by some of the over-elaborate outfits he was wearing.

The Summer Festival began in Las Vegas on August 18 1975, but three days later, Elvis was back in Memphis in hospital with fatigue. The shows were rescheduled for December, at which time Elvis flew to Vegas in his new acquisition, a Convair 880 jetliner he'd had customised and had named *Lisa Marie*. He'd also bought a smaller Jet Star plane, and was having a racquetball court built at Graceland to cater for his interest in the sport. (In 1976, he planned to open a chain of raquetball [similar to the game of squash] courts across the Southern US called "Presley Centre Courts", but later cancelled his plans.)

Right: In December 1976 The "Getaway" Trophy was taken to Las Vegas for Elvis by British Fan Club boss Todd Slaughter and Elvis proudly showed it to his Hilton audience. (Dave Reynolds)

BACK ON FORM

Fans who saw shows at the Hilton between December 2 and 15 reported that Elvis was looking much healthier. He was playing one show a night, with two on Saturdays. Voice had disbanded, but their tenor, Shaun Nielsen, remained with Elvis.

On Christmas Day, Elvis took friends for a flight in the *Lisa Marie* and gave them all jewellery, and on New Year's

Eve, played a concert at the gigantic Silverdome at Pontiac, Michigan, for over 60,000 fans, setting a new box office record of $800,000.

It was the USA's Bicentennial and he sang 'America The Beautiful

Below: Ed Parker was head of the Kempo Karate Institute. He was considered as a God by his followers but chose to act as a body guard for no fee for Elvis whilst on tour. A Hawaiian Mormon, young Ed Parker was the child who first alerted the U.S. Coast Guard to the approach of Japanese aircraft which were about to bomb Pearl Harbor. (Ed Parker Estate)

After a vacation in Vail, a winter sports resort in Colorado, in January 1976, Elvis agreed to RCA recording at Graceland. The Jungle Room was turned into a recording studio and between February 2 and 7, a dozen tracks were cut. The resulting album, *From Elvis Presley Boulevard, Memphis, Tennessee*, was criticised for its downbeat mood with songs like 'The Last Farewell' and 'Hurt'. There was a heartfelt 'Danny Boy' and a haunting 'Blue Eyes Crying In The Rain'. Downbeat or not,

the album showcased Elvis's artistry. 'Hurt' was released as a single, and it was a highlight of many concerts. Another song cut at Graceland, 'Moody Blue', became a big hit later in the year. There was a second, short session at Graceland in October.

Elvis did tour after tour in 1976 – nine in all, revisiting Lake Tahoe, and playing the Hilton in December. It was the USA's Bicentennial and when he sang 'America The Beautiful', audiences everywhere responded enthusiastically. For much of the year, he wore outfits known as the "Bicentennial Suits" and looked a little trimmer. Long-time pianist Glen Hardin left, and was replaced by Tony Brown. David Briggs joined the band on electric piano, which was used to great effect when Elvis sang 'Love Letters'.

In what would be his final Las Vegas season, Elvis gave fifteen shows between December 2 and 12. Fans who saw all the shows could see that all was not as it should be. After a very good, long

Right: Todd Slaughter met Elvis for the last time on June 26, 1977 at Indianapolis Airport. Todd received an award for being (at that time) British fan club secretary for 10 years. RCA's George Parkhill looks on. This was the last official photograph taken of Elvis Presley. Seven weeks later on 16, August 1977 Elvis died at his Memphis Mansion Graceland. (EPFC)

opening show, Elvis began to look unwell, especially around the eyes; very little sparkle remained. On December 5, he limped on stage saying he'd fallen in his bedroom. There was concern that he might not complete the season but he did and despite the problems, Elvis's voice never let him down. He'd long ago lost interest in singing the early hits

For all his health problems, however, his glorious voice stayed true to the end of his life

and usually rushed through them, but he sang 'Tryin' To Get To You' and 'Blue Christmas' well, and turned in some droll versions of 'Are You Lonesome Tonight' directed by Charlie Hodge. The previous month, Linda Thompson had finally left Elvis and accompanying him in Vegas on this visit was his new girlfriend, Ginger Alden. A short tour in late December found Elvis in great form, and the year ended on a high note with a concert at Pittsburgh on December 31.

During 1976, three of Elvis's long-term bodyguards had been dismissed by Vernon Presley, partly for reasons of economy and partly because, in the litigation-mad culture that was sweeping America, their over-aggressive behaviour had resulted in embarrassing lawsuits. The disgruntled trio, Red and Sonny West and Dave Hebler, announced their intention of writing a tell-all book with tabloid journalist Steve Dunleavy. It seemed as if the privacy that Elvis had long since enjoyed with regard to his private life was about to dissolve in a welter of shocking headlines.

Right: "The Final Curtain" Elvis Presley reads the words of 'My Way' at his final show in Indianapolis on June 26, 1977 (Dave Reynolds)

A planned recording session in January, 1977 at new Nashville studio, Creative Workshop was cancelled when Elvis pleaded a sore throat. He toured eastern states in February, then took Ginger and several friends to Hawaii in March. Their stay at a beach house at Kailua was cut short when Elvis got sand in his eye and flew home.

The next tour got underway, but Elvis became ill at the end of March and cancelled shows, spending a few days in Baptist Hospital. The tours continued; at Baltimore on May 29, there were more concerns after Elvis left the stage for 30 minutes during his show.

Despite all Elvis's health problems, Col Parker did a deal with CBS for a TV special. Elvis was filmed at a lacklustre show in Omaha, Nebraska on June 19, and at Rapid City, South Dakota, two days later. The British Fan Club flew out to see shows at Cincinnati and Indianapolis on June 25 and 26, witnessing what would be Elvis's final concerts. The Indianapolis show was a long one, and Elvis was in sparkling form. Todd Slaughter was filmed with him at Indianapolis airport prior to the show which turned out to be the last footage of Elvis ever to be shot.

His tour over, Elvis returned to Memphis, and Lisa Marie joined him at Graceland on July 31, and he rented out the former fairgrounds, Libertyland, for her and her friends. The bodyguards' book, titled *Elvis: What Happened?*, was published on August 4, and detailed amongst other things Elvis's addiction to prescription drugs.

THE FINAL HOURS

In the early hours of August 16, Elvis played racquetball, then sat at his piano and sang a few songs before retiring. Around lunchtime, Ginger awoke, and found Elvis collapsed in his bathroom. Paramedics were called and he was rushed to Baptist Hospital, but it was too late. The news flashed round the world that Elvis Presley was dead of a probable heart attack, and fans were in shock.

By the time the funeral was held on August 18, after a "lying-in-state" at Graceland, record stores worldwide were rapidly running out of Presley product, and tributes were pouring in. Elvis was laid to rest in a mausoleum at Forest Hill Cemetery, but permission was granted for him and his mother to be moved to Graceland's Meditation Garden. On October 2, their caskets were brought back home.

The next evening, CBS screened *Elvis In Concert* and viewers were shocked to see how ill Elvis had looked. For all his health problems, however, his glorious voice stayed true to the end of his life.

R LINES
AIR LINES
AIR LINES
AIR LINES
TA AIR LINES
DELTA AIR LINES
THE COL

EPILOGUE

Almost three decades after his death, the legend of Elvis Presley lives on. Elvis may have been dead now for over a quarter of a century but creative marketing, simple curiosity and the sheer thrill of hearing his singing voice keep the memory and name alive in all four corners of the earth. Having achieved unprecedented record sales during his lifetime, and in death surpassing those totals, Elvis is the pop music icon whose legacy remains the yardstick for all present and future acts. Make no mistake Elvis is here to stay – today, tomorrow and forever.

Elvis left his entire estate, believed to have been less than $5 million, to his daughter Lisa Marie, in trust until she reached her 25th birthday. Priscilla was appointed co-executor of Elvis's will and it is largely through her enterprise and clear-sighted business sense that the Elvis industry has prospered so successfully since his death. The estate is now worth well over $100 million.

Memphis, of course, is the hub of most Elvis activity, and a Mecca for fans, especially in January for birthday celebrations and in August for *Elvis Week* with its candlelight vigil. From late November, 1977, fans were allowed to visit Elvis's gravesite in the Meditation Garden, and in June, 1982, Graceland was opened as a museum, and draws 600,000 visitors annually. The ground and lower floors are included on the tour, plus the back yard. The amazing Trophy Room cannot fail to impress, and the Racquetball Court now houses many recent disc awards. Horses still graze the back pasture. There's no commercial activity within the grounds – that's all across the boulevard in Elvis Presley Plaza. Elvis's grave never lacks floral tributes. His father and grandmother are buried here, too, alongside Gladys.

Left: Colonel Parker awaits for the arrival of his star to perform for the very last time. (EPFC)

Elvis's name and image is everywhere. There have been hundreds of books – good and bad – magazines, and articles. There have been stage musicals, videos, DVDs, documentaries, biographical movies, exhibitions, and auctions. There have been hundreds of fan socials, conventions, memorial tours, and holidays. The TCB Band (Elvis's 1970s musicians), have toured the world with the "Virtual Elvis" concert. There have been bootlegs and out-takes, compilations and remixes of Elvis's music, with a remix of 'A Little Less Conversation' from 1968 making No 1 in the UK in June, 2002. Archivists Ernst Jorgensen and

Elvis will live on via his music and influence on generations of performers

Roger Semon have done wonders with Elvis's catalogue since the early Nineties, producing multiple CD box-sets in elaborate packages with an attention to detail that contrasts sharply with almost everything produced during Elvis's lifetime. His music still sells, big time.

Elvis statues grace several cities around the world. Souvenirs and memorabilia of every description have tempted fans to part with their money. TV commercials using his music, image or name appear often. Countless "tribute artists" perform, some successfully. Elvis websites abound, and many fans work tirelessly for charity in his name.

The key people in Elvis's life are gone: Vernon died in 1979, Col Parker in 1997, JD Sumner in 1998, and Sam Phillips in 2003, plus many more who played their part in the Elvis story.

Elvis will live on via his music and influence on generations of performers. And for his fans, without an *Elvis* song, the day will never end.

CREDITS

Thanks

The authors would like to thank Rita Nixon, Richard Harvey, and Janice Scott (Tupelo) for help and encouragement.

Main Reference Sources

Elvis Day By Day (Peter Guralnick/Ernst Jorgensen)
A Life In Music – The Complete Recording Sessions (Ernst Jorgensen)
Elvis Word For Word (Jerry Osborne)
Elvis, The Concert Years 1969-1977 (Stein Erik Skar)

Our Photographic Content

During his lifetime Elvis Presley was photographed more times, we believe, than any other star in the world of entertainment. I would like to thank all our picture source researchers for their efforts in providing us with some of the rarest shots of Elvis Presley that were taken over the years with some of the world's greatest celebrities. Special thanks go to Pal Granlund (Flaming Star EPFC Norway - which boasts the largest Presley picture archive outside of the US), Joe A Tunzi (JAT Publishing, Chicago), Jean-Marie Pouzenc (Elvis: My Happiness Fan Club of Paris), Jean-Marc Gargiullo (Treat Me Nice EPFC of France), MGM, Universal, Paramount, Hal. B Wallis, Colonel Tom Parker, Tom Jones, Dave Reynolds, Sir Jimmy Savile, OBE, KCSG, and the official Elvis Presley Fan Club of Great Britain Picture Archive.

Right: Faron Young with his wife with Elvis at the Grand Ole Opry on December 21, 1957 (Granlund)
Following pages: Liberace with Elvis in Las Vegas 1956 (Granlund)

About The Authors

Anne E Nixon has been an Elvis fan since 1956, and saw 40 Presley shows at the Las Vegas Hilton between 1972 and 76. She has written hundreds of articles for Elvis magazines all over the world. In 1986, her book, *Elvis, Ten Years After* was published. She is a contributing editor of the magazine of the Official Elvis Presley Fan Club of Great Britain. Anne lives in Dudley in the West Midlands.

Todd Slaughter has been involved with the official Elvis Presley Fan Club since 1962 and took over as president on 16th August 1967 – ten years prior to Elvis's death. He met Elvis in 1972, 1973 and in 1977, and had an excellent relationship with Elvis' manager Colonel Tom Parker. Outside of the Elvis world Slaughter, a mechanical engineer, has edited and published a series of magazines notably CB News and Satellite TV News – both of which spearheaded the changes in communications and broadcasting in the UK.

As a broadcaster Todd Slaughter has appeared on most major networks around the world, and can presently be heard on SAGA 106.6FM co-hosting the Elvis hour with veteran presenter and SAGA Radio director Ron Coles.

About The Fan Club

The official Elvis Presley Fan Club of Great Britain is the world's largest. There is an active membership of 20,000 and the club's magazines are shipped around the world. The British fan base has a network of Branch Leaders across the country. The club operates trips to Memphis and elsewhere in the US twice each year, hosts week long Elvis themed holiday functions in the UK, and occasionally teams up with its European partners to stage international conventions across Europe.

For further details write to: EPFC, PO Box 4, Leicester, LE1 3ZL, England
Visit: www.elvisweb.co.uk